CU00703875

The Story of India's Freedom Movement

Nayantara Sahgal is the author of nine novels, six works of non-fiction and wide-ranging literary and political commentary. She has received the Sahitya Akademi Award, the Sinclair Prize and the Commonwealth Writers' Prize. She is a member of the American Academy of Arts and Sciences, has a Distinguished Alumna Award from Wellesley College, USA, and Woodstock School, India, and an Honorary Doctorate of Letters from the University of Leeds. In 2011, she received the Nanjanagudu Thirumalamba Award for her contribution to Indian literature, and in 2009, Zee TV's Awadh Samman. A resident of Dehradun, she has also been awarded the Doon Ratna.

The Story of India's Freedom Movement

Nayantara Sahgal

Illustrations by
Sayantan Halder

RED TURTLE
RUPA

Published in Red Turtle by
Rupa Publications India Pvt. Ltd. 2013
7/16, Ansari Road, Daryaganj
New Delhi 110002

Sales Centres:

Allahabad Bengaluru Chennai
Hyderabad Jaipur Kathmandu
Kolkata Mumbai

First published by National Council of
Educational Research and Training, 1970

ISBN: 978-81-291-2116-5

10 9 8 7 6 5 4 3 2 1

The moral right of the author has been asserted.

Typeset in Book Antiqua 12.5/19.2

Printed by Replika Press Pvt. Ltd., Haryana

Contents

The Idea of Freedom

We take our freedom for granted. We understand now that every person is important, that each person is different from all others and has the right to decide for himself how his life is to be led. Yet it was not always natural to believe this. There was a time when slavery was accepted as a natural state of affairs. Some men were free and others slaves, and no one thought this strange. In ancient Italy, for example, there were three slaves for every free man. The free men lived in comfort and governed the land. The slaves laboured on plantations and in households, and were often brutally treated by their masters. In every ancient civilization, it was the slaves' hard work that built great monuments and made progress possible.

There is a famous statue of a Scythian slave sharpening a knife. His body is bent and he seems to represent the suffering of millions in the past. Yet he is looking upward, as if towards the light, reminding us that the longing to be free is as old as the institution of slavery.

There was never a time when men did not yearn to be free. History is full of stirring examples of this urge. One of the earliest and most dramatic of these is the slave uprising that took place in the Roman Empire in 73 BCE. It was led by Spartacus, a slave who escaped from a school for gladiators at Capua. He fled to Mount Vesuvius, where he collected an army of runaway slaves like himself. For two years, he and his followers put up a desperate fight, defeating every army that Rome sent against them, but the rebellion was finally crushed. Spartacus was killed and six thousand of his followers were crucified along the Appian Way in Rome.

There are countless examples of men like Spartacus who fought to free themselves from oppression. There were others — thinkers, philosophers and scientists — who fought for freedom of the mind and spirit from the tyranny of the. rigid beliefs of their time. Socrates, the Athenian, was condemned to death because he would not give up his right to speak what he believed was the truth. Galileo, to whom modern physics owes its beginnings, was the first astronomer to use a telescope. He saw the mountains and craters on the moon, discovered four satellites of Jupiter, and realized that the Milky Way is a collection of stars. We know all these as facts now, but in 1632, they were considered heresy, that is, going against the beliefs of the Christian church. Galileo was called before the religious court. He was made to go down on his knees and take back what he believed, and sentenced to live a lonely, isolated life. But he continued to work on his discoveries till he died ten years later.

It is because of men and women like these, and their determination to live and think freely no matter what, that the struggle for freedom has gone on through history. Because of them, we can take freedom for granted today and believe that it is our right to exercise it. Yet, individual freedom cannot be properly exercised if a country is not free. Every country has its own heritage and achievements of which it is proud, which it wants to pass on to each new generation. Every country is best fitted to make plans for its own future, because it is more concerned with its people's needs than any foreign government can ever be. Only in a free country can men and women direct their lives and achieve the best of which they are capable.

Galileo

But freedom from a foreign power, or political freedom, is only a starting point. The greatest Indian of our time, Mahatma Gandhi, believed that freedom would be a reality only when we had succeeded in wiping the tear from every eye, and when every citizen has the opportunity to live with dignity.

This book tells the story of India's struggle for freedom. To understand it we have to go back in time to more than two hundred years ago. We must begin with the establishment of British rule on our soil, discover how a foreign power became so dominant in our country, and then trace the efforts that brought us our independence.

The British Come to India

The Fall of the Mughal Empire

The year was 1707. Aurangzeb, the last of the great Mughal emperors, was dead and the stage was set for a struggle to seize the prize he had left: India. There was no single power strong enough to take it. Aurangzeb's own descendants were too weak to exercise any real authority. The Marathas and the Sikhs were steadily growing in power and eyeing the prize and so were two nations from across the seas—England and France—who had also become increasingly powerful.

The English and the French had come to India as merchants but had become involved with the quarrels of local rulers. For example, whenever there was a disputed succession in the South, the English would back one candidate to the throne, and the French the other, and both would lend out their trained troops to the warring sides. After the war, they would seize whatever they could in wealth and territory.

At this time, invaders were also waiting beyond India's north-west frontier, ready to march down into the rich plains and plunder. It was a time of trouble and turmoil, and an ideal opportunity for adventurers, both Indian and foreign.

In 1739, one of the contenders for the prize, Nadir Shah, king of Persia, swept down with his armies in one of the most terrible invasions North India had ever known. He spread death and destruction on a savage scale, emptied the Mughal treasury and shook the very foundations of the empire. Within seventeen years, Ahmad Shah Abdali, the Afghan, began his raids, and in 1761 he defeated the Maratha army at Panipat. He returned to his own country only when a revolt broke out there. North India lay trampled under these invasions.

The Rise of the East India Company

Meanwhile, in 1757, the English had taken possession of Bengal. They had made an attempt to do so during Aurangzeb's reign but had been

East India Company soldiers in uniform

badly defeated. This time they succeeded. Siraj-ud-Daula, the Nawab of Bengal, was an incompetent ruler and no match in ambition,

East India Company coins

daring or intrigue for the Englishman, Robert Clive, an official of the East India Company. Clive bribed the Nawab's minister, Mir Jafar, to turn traitor and side with the English. Having prepared the ground in this way and by forging a document to strengthen his plot, Clive marched out of Calcutta and defeated the Nawab in battle at Plassey. This was a small battle in which the English victory was due more to treachery than to superior arms, but it had important results. It laid the foundation of the British Empire in India.

The East India Company, begun as a body of London merchants with a trading charter from Queen Elizabeth, now had control of the revenues of Bengal. Its officials used these to make huge fortunes for themselves. A few years later, in 1764, the Company won another battle at Buxar, this time against Mir Qasim, son-in-law of the deposed Mir Jafar, and the weak Mughal Emperor Shah Alam who had come to his aid. The battle of Buxar made the English masters of both Bengal and Bihar and reduced the Emperor in Delhi to the position of a puppet.

Meanwhile, the English had also triumphed over their rivals, the French, in the South. They were able to do so chiefly because the East India Company had the backing of the British Parliament and government. In addition, the English navy enjoyed supremacy at sea and could therefore prevent the French from providing additional support to their land forces. By 1761, the French had lost their influence in India and their possessions were reduced to Chandernagar, Pondicherry and Mahe. The British had triumphed over their powerful rivals.

The Maratha Warriors

As the central authority in Delhi grew weaker, it became less able to cope with the growing strength of the Marathas. A Maratha chieftain named Shahji Bhonsle had been a source of anxiety to the Mughals since the reign of Shah Jahan. He was succeeded by his son, Shivaji, a brilliant leader who became a legend among his people and inspired the respect of even his enemies.

Shivaji founded the Maratha Empire. The Mughal officials in the South were so afraid of him that they paid him a tribute to protect themselves. This payment was known as 'chauth' or fourth part of revenue.

The Marathas claimed this 'chauth' from all the territories they conquered, and even the Delhi Emperor had to recognize their right to do so.

Shivaji's son, Sambhaji, was captured and killed by the Mughals, but the Maratha power continued to grow until their defeat at Panipat in 1761. This stopped their rise for some years until they recovered and were once again the most formidable power in India.

Gradually, the Peshwa or Prime Minister, became the real Maratha ruler while the Raja took second place, and several chieftains, all dependants of the Peshwa, emerged as separate rulers. The most famous of these were the Scindia of Gwalior, the the Gaekwar of Baroda and the Holkar of Indore. Jealousies and rivalries grew between them and they were not able to unite against their common enemy, the English.

The Maratha power collapsed with the death of its two most able leaders, Mahadji Scindia of Gwalior in 1794 and Nana Farnavis, the Chief Minister of the Peshwa at Poona, in 1799. The English took advantage of the rivalries among the Maratha rulers and inflicted war upon them, annexing their kingdoms in 1819.

Tipu, the Tiger of the Deccan

There was still one more power to contend with in the South. This was Haider Ali of Mysore who defeated the British in battle again and again. After his death, his son, Tipu Sultan, continued to oppose them. It took a triple alliance of the English, the Marathas and the Nizam of

Hyderabad to overthrow Tipu, and the three allies carved up his kingdom among themselves. It took still another war, the Fourth Mysore War, to destroy Tipu completely. This time, in 1799, his capital Seringapatam (Srirangapatna) was stormed and Tipu fell fighting.

Tipu's hatred for the British is epitomized in the mechanical toy that he ordered to be made especially for his court. It shows a wooden tiger killing a model

of a European man. A special mechanism inside the toy made the dying man wail, and move one of his arms, while the tiger grunted. Additionally, a flap on the side of the tiger opened to reveal a small pipe organ with eighteen notes.

The Sikhs

The English came in contact with the Sikhs in the early nineteenth century although the Sikhs had been a power to reckon with for some time before that. They had begun as a peaceful sect interested in religious matters, until Jahangir had Arjun Singh—the fifth Guru, who compiled the Granth—arrested and killed for political offence. Later Aurangzeb ordered the ninth Guru, Tegh Bahadur, to embrace Islam and when he refused, put him to death.

It was under the tenth Guru, Govind Singh, that the Sikhs became a powerful military community, mainly to oppose Aurangzeb. By the end of the eighteenth century, a Sikh state had emerged in Punjab under the great leader, Ranjit Singh. The English were friendly with him and were bound by treaty to respect the boundary between his territory and theirs. But after his death, when his kingdom fell into disorder, they took advantage of the confusion and occupied Punjab in the course of two wars.

India Under the East India Company

The East India Company now ruled large areas of India and under the pretext of trade, carried away vast amounts of India's wealth.

The greed of its officials brought misery to the people and, to add to this, one-third of the population died of starvation in a famine in 1770. The Company took no measures to relieve the suffering of the people and continued to collect the full amount of land revenue.

In 1772, five years after Clive's departure from India, Warren Hastings arrived as the Governor of Bengal. He later became the first Governor-General of the Company's possessions in India. Both Clive and Hastings, on their return to England, were accused of corrupt practices by the British Parliament. Clive was censured and he committed suicide. Hastings was acquitted after a long trial. But though they had been severely criticized, were greatly admired by their countrymen as the founders of the British Empire in India.

After Hastings and until the revolt of 1857, a succession of English Governors-General ruled the Company's possessions. Of these, some followed an openly aggressive policy. They waged wars and annexed territories till almost all of India came under their rule. Then they advanced beyond its frontiers to attack Burma, Afghanistan and Nepal. These wars were a drain on India's finances. Dalhousie, the last Governor-General before the revolt of 1857, had a three-sided policy of annexation. He based it first of all on the right of conquest; second, on the belief that British rule should replace the inefficient rule of local rulers in some of the Indian states; and third, on the Doctrine of Lapse. According to this doctrine, he would seize territories still under Indian rule if the ruler died without leaving a natural heir. As the right to adopt an heir had existed in Indian states for hundreds of years before the British came, the Indian rulers resented this policy.

While the conquests and annexations went on, some Governors-General introduced new administrative measures. Cornwallis, who followed Hastings, started a system of revenue collection called the Permanent Settlement. Under this system, zamindars were to act as middlemen between the government and the peasants. It was easier for the Company to deal with its own chosen loyal supporters than with a vast peasantry. But the system was hard on the peasant who began to live in fear of the zamindar and his harsh methods of collecting revenue. If he could not pay the zamindar, he had to borrow from the village moneylender, and so got deeper and deeper into debt, often losing all or part of his land holdings. The number of peasants without land began to grow. What had been for the English a convenient way of collecting revenue became a tragedy for India.

A noted administrator was Bentinck, the first Governor-General to act on the principle that the English had a duty to improve the welfare of their Indian subjects. His famous reforms were the abolition of sati—though there had been an agitation for this much earlier by the Indian reformer Raja Ram Mohan Roy—and the suppression of the thuggees. It was also in Bentinck's time that a decision was taken that had far-reaching consequences for India. In 1835, it was decided that the medium of higher education would be English and that the funds granted by the government for education would be used only for the study of English and the Western sciences.

Sati was a Hindu practice in which women burnt themselves on the pyres of their dead husbands. Since, obviously, many did not want to do so willingly, they were forced by cruel relatives who did not want to accept the 'burden' of looking after a widow. Thuggees were groups of assassins who roamed the countryside from as far back as the fourteenth century. They would join groups of travellers and later kill them for their valuables by strangling them.

The Decline of Indian Industries

During its years of rule, the Company was able to establish a firm economic hold on India. It had originally come to buy the fine Indian articles that were supplied to Asian and European markets since ancient times. For nearly two thousand years India had held a proud and unrivalled position in the world's trade. At first, the Company encouraged Indian industries because it made money out of them, but English manufacturers did not like this competition. They persuaded their Parliament to tax Indian goods coming to England, while English goods entered India without paying duty. Gradually this policy halted India's industrial development, making it a purely agricultural country that would supply raw materials for English factories, while English machine-made goods began to flood the Indian markets. Indian industries slowly collapsed. The textile industry was the first to decline, followed by ship-building, metal work, glass and paper. Millions of artisans and craftsmen were thrown out of work and into conditions of suffering and starvation.

As the nineteenth century progressed, the English built roads and railways which transported English goods all over India and took Indian raw material to ports for shipment overseas. India's once flourishing industries were slowly but steadily ruined. Workmen began to leave the cities and go back to their villages to try and earn a living from agriculture, but there were already too many people trying to make a livelihood from the land.

The Revolt of 1857

Beginnings of Discontent

Dalhousie's Doctrine of Lapse had stirred the anger of the Indian states and many rulers were bitter at the treatment they had received. Three Maratha states, Satara, Jhansi and Nagpur, had been annexed, and later, Oudh (Awadh) as well. Dalhousie stopped the pension given to the deposed Peshwa, Baji Rao, and to his son, Nana Sahib. The ruling houses now began to be afraid for their future security. In Awadh, the landowning classes were angry at the deposition of the ruler and at the way they had been treated after the annexation. There was also a general fear that with the spread of English education and the missionary activity encouraged by the government, India's old religions and traditions were in danger. Both Hindus and Muslims rallied to this cry. A revolt was organized that was to take place around Uttar Pradesh and central India. Its aim was to throw out foreign power and bring back the Mughal Emperor as the ruler. It was not a revolt of the common people, but many joined in because they could relate to the hardships of the Company's rule.

The sepoys, or the native Indian soldiers in the East India Company, grew gradually discontented with their British officers, but what triggered the revolt was the Enfield Rifle issued to the sepoys, the cartridges of which were rumoured to be greased with pork fat. The sepoys had to bite the cartridge open to load the rifle. Many of them refused, as touching pork was against their religion. The British refused to give in to religious prejudice, which added fuel to the fire.

A date was fixed for the rebellion to start simultaneously in several places, but some Indian regiments at Meerut rebelled earlier than planned, on 10 May 1857. Within forty-eight hours, Delhi had fallen to the rebels and they proclaimed the feeble old Bahadur Shah, last of the Mughal line, Emperor of India. The Meerut rebellion flared and spread. There were similar outbreaks all over North and Central India and, between the months of May and September 1857, English authority hung by a slender thread in several places across the country.

There was terrible bloodshed on both sides and numerous grim events of the revolt have been told and retold ever since. One of these is the siege of Lucknow. On the 30th of June, when the English were defeated outside Lucknow (then capital of Awadh), the Europeans in the city took shelter in the Residency, the home of the English Resident, and held out with courage and endurance under a long siege, until it was finally lifted in November. The names of Generals Outram and Havelock who fought their way into the Residency are associated with this ordeal as examples of how bravely the English fought against great odds.

Meanwhile, in Cawnpore (Kanpur), Englishmen, women and children were massacred. The English avenged this outrage when they recaptured Delhi in September. They spread terror over the city, looting and killing in cold blood. 'All the people found within the walls when our

The Lucknow Siege, 1857

troops entered were bayoneted on the spot,' wrote Lord Canning, the Governor-General. General Neill, marching from Allahabad to Kanpur, laid waste villages and hanged people along the way till there was hardly a tree by the roadside that did not have a victim. The ruthless way in which the uprising was crushed lived on in the memory of Indians for generations afterwards.

In the end, the revolt failed. It was the first organized uprising against the English but it was fought for a lost cause: the re-establishment of the old feudal order. It wanted to restore the Mughal Emperor, whose power had long since been a fiction. Mughal glory had vanished and no rebellion could restore it. Besides, the revolt did not have the support of all the states. The Gurkhas, sent by Nepal, and the Sikhs sided with the English, as did the Nizam in the south and Scindia in the North. And it was because the Indian troops in Punjab made common cause with the English that they were able to besiege and recapture Delhi in September 1857.

*The fall of Delhi was not the end of the
revolt. Rani Laxmibai of Jhansi, a young
widow of twenty, held out heroically against the
English forces, leading her troops into
battle even after her fort was captured
in April 1858. She was described by the
English General who opposed her as 'the best
and bravest' of the rebel leaders. She died
fighting and later, her General, Tantia Tope,
continued to harass the English until
his betrayal and execution in 1859.*

The revolt brought about the end of the Mughal dynasty. The aged Bahadur Shah, descendant of the proud line of Babur, was exiled to Rangoon, and his two sons were shot. The rule of the East India Company also came to an end and the British Crown now took direct control of India. Under the new system the Governor- General was now called Viceroy. In the place of the Company's Directors, a Secretary of State for India with a council of fifteen members was made responsible for Indian affairs. These changes were announced to the people of India by proclamation on 1 November 1858. It outlined the principles on which the Crown would govern India. The ruling princes, it said, would be assured of their rights. There would be religious tolerance, and the rebels, except those who had taken part in the murder of British subjects, would be pardoned.

England and India now clearly entered a new phase in their relationship—the ruler and the ruled. The construction of the Suez Canal in 1869 made direct communication possible between the two countries, and the Secretary of State began to exercise almost unlimited power over India's affairs. In 1877, Queen Victoria of England took the title of 'Empress of India'.

The Legacy of the Revolt

The revolt of 1857 had a profound effect on the English and on their attitude towards India. During the past hundred years they had extended their rule over India and established an administrative system. They had grown in power and confidence. The revolt shook this confidence and suddenly they realized the danger that surrounded them. They knew they could never again relax their watchfulness in the country they had conquered by force and which they ruled with the might of their superior military arms. They were certain that a popular united movement, determined to get rid of them, could succeed; they had to take care that this did not happen. A trading company could no longer protect their interests. The British government, which now took direct charge, had to rely even more heavily on its military strength. They became even more suspicious and distrustful of Indians and had less and less social contact with them. The Englishman's life began to be confined to his home, his office and his club. The Indians and the English began to live in virtual isolation from each other.

Apart from the economic advantages the possession of India brought them, Englishmen sincerely believed they had the task of civilizing this country, that it was their duty. They compared the British Empire to the Roman Empire which had brought the benefits of law and order to 'backward' people, and they felt they had the same mission to fulfil. They were dedicated to this task. It seems strange to us today that one nation should feel ordained to rule another, yet the words of leading Englishmen of that time make it clear to us how passionately they believed in their mission.

In a letter to the *Times* on 4 January 1878, James Fitzjames Stephen wrote, '...I deny that ambition and conquest are crimes; I say that ambition is the great incentive to every manly virtue, and that conquest is the process by which every great state in the world has been built up... I, for one, feel no shame when I think of the great competitive examination which has lasted for a hundred years and of which the first paper was set upon the field of Plassey, and the last (for the present) under the walls of Delhi and Lucknow...'

In 1888 Sir John Strachey wrote '...there never was a country, and never will be, in which the government of foreigners is really popular. It will be the beginning and end of our Empire when we forget this elementary fact and entrust the greater executive powers to the hands of the natives... It is clear that the only hope for India is the long continuance of the benevolent but strong government of Englishmen.'

The verses of the poet, Rudyard Kipling, reached the English masses even more eloquently. It was he who coined the famous phrase, 'White Man's burden', and made it the slogan of a whole era:

> Take up the White Man's burden
> And reap his old reward:
> The blame of those ye better,
> The hate of those ye guard—

Kipling's poem meant that however dreary the task, however unpopular its doer, it was the white man's sacred duty to govern and civilize India. It was in this mood and crusading spirit that the nineteenth-century Englishman took up the reins of the government of India.

When the British Crown took over, there were immediate changes from the way in which the East India Company had governed the country.

First, Dalhousie's Doctrine of Lapse was given up. About two-fifths of the country, consisting of some seven hundred states, still lay outside British India. These states were allowed to remain under their ruling princes but there was a British Resident posted in each state, without whose approval the ruler could do little.

A second change was brought about by the Indian Councils Act of 1861. A number of Indians, including two ruling princes, were associated with the work of lawmaking in the provinces. This step was taken as a way of keeping the government informed of opinion in the country, and of warning it in time to prevent any discontent from erupting into rebellion.

A third change was the reorganization of the army. The English believed that the revolt had become possible because the number of Europeans in the armed forces was not adequate as compared to that of the Indians. The European element was increased and the Indian soldiers were cut down in number.

A new era had begun, but before we go on to other political events, we must go back to see what impression English ideas and education made on India and how they influenced Indian ways of living and thinking.

The Stir of Ideas

New Thoughts and Ideas

The coming of the English had far-reaching effects on India. One of these was the expansion of English education during Bentinck's administration. It proved to be the first step towards independence because it gave rise to a new English-educated professional class of people — lawyers, businessmen, journalists and professors, who would eventually become the leaders of the national movement. English became a common language for upper-class Indians and through it, a feeling of unity and nationalism slowly developed. Macaulay, who fathered this scheme of education, can be regarded as one of the founders of modern India.

What Macaulay did was revolutionary. He planned the conquest of India through the English language. Until then, the many invaders who entered India had been absorbed into the Indian fabric of life. Macaulay saw English education as a means of absorbing India into the English way of life. He believed that Indians would thus become attached to British ideas and institutions. Independent India has shown this attachment by adopting the British parliamentary system of government and by the continued use of the English language. Macaulay also believed that the teaching of Christianity in schools and colleges would eventually lead to a widespread acceptance of Christianity in India. But in this he was proved wrong.

By 1857, universities had been established at Calcutta (Kolkata), Bombay (Mumbai) and Madras (Chennai), but even before this, the rapid spread of English brought vital new currents of thought to India from the Western world. In Europe, this was an age of intellectual advancement that was bringing about great changes in Western society. These ideas began to stimulate Indian thinking. Bengal took the lead in this stir of ideas. Indians began to re-examine their age-old beliefs and realized that some of these needed changing. The challenge of the West affected the Hindu religion, too, and led to a great reforming zeal that became the spiritual background for later political action.

The First Reformers and the Reinvention of Hinduism

The first of the reformers was Raja Ram Mohan Roy, the most distinguished Hindu of his time. **Ram Mohan Roy** (1772-1833) was born and brought up a Brahmin, but he was educated — like all Hindus who wanted to enter public service — in Islamic culture and was a scholar of Arabic and Persian. After he entered the service of the East India Company, he began to study English, which opened the world of Western thought to him. Christianity attracted him greatly, too, and he made a serious study of Hebrew and

Greek in order to understand it better. After much study and heart-searching, he decided that what his people needed was not Christianity, but a new understanding of their own traditions. His decision led to the beginning of the

Raja Ram Mohan Roy

Hindu reformation, without which India could not have emerged as a modern nation. In 1828, he founded the Brahmo Samaj, an organization through which he tried to combine Western ideas with the philosophy of the Hindu scriptures.

Hinduism at the beginning of the nineteenth century was at a low ebb. It had many scriptures but no single authority to unite all Hindus in their thinking. It consisted of a variety of customs, many of which had become meaningless with the passage of time. Its laws, codified two thousand years ago, were considered sacred and unchangeable. It had become a religion largely concerned with ritual. Its social institutions like caste and the joint family had become rigid, and evil practices had crept into its working. In its stagnant condition it could provide no light or inspiration for progress.

Ram Mohan Roy saw the depths to which Hinduism had sunk in Bengal. His Brahmo Samaj was founded to cleanse Hinduism of superstition, to fight the evils of caste, polygamy and other customs, to raise the status of women, and to bring a modern, Westernized approach to India's problems. The crusading spirit of the Brahmo Samaj soon spread, and in Bombay in 1867, Keshub Chandra Sen founded the Prarthana Samaj on similar lines, with special emphasis on reform. One of its well-known members was Mahadev Govind Ranade, who was later associated with the founding of the Indian National Congress.

A wave of reform entered Hinduism from another direction too. **Swami Dayanand Saraswati** established the Arya Samaj in Punjab with the purpose of uniting all Hindus under the philosophy of the Vedas. He believed that the Vedas represented the highest doctrines of Hinduism. India, he felt, could only be reborn through the revival of her ancient Hindu ideals. His movement was quite militant in its efforts to bring non-Hindus into the fold.

The Vedanta movement found its greatest leader in **Swami Vivekananda**, a disciple of the saintly Ramakrishna Paramahansa. Ramakrishna was one of the most extraordinary men of his time, a poor, uneducated priest who became a divinely inspired teacher, practising different religions to show that they were all equal before God. His disciple, Vivekananda, founded the Ramakrishna Mission to carry on his master's teachings.

Vivekananda believed that the Vedas had a message not only for Hindus but for all mankind. He trained a body of missionaries to spread this message and Vedanta philosophy became known all over the world. Vivekananda's magnetic personality also made a vivid impression on his countrymen and on those he met on his journeys abroad. He strongly urged Hindus to rise above the religion of the 'cooking pots' and to live according to the fearless and noble ideals of the Vedas. His lectures and writings rejuvenated his audiences and shocked them out of their apathy. Educated Hindus realized they had a heritage to be proud of and that there was no need to be apologetic about their religion. By the end of the nineteenth century and in the first twenty years of the twentieth century, the movement grew in strength and Vedanta became widely accepted as the background of all Hindu thought.

A famous example of Swami Vivekananda's influence across the world is the instance of his speech at the Parliament of the World's Religions in Chicago in 1893. In his opening speech, Vivekananda addressed all those who were assembled there as 'Sisters and Brothers of America', to which he got a standing ovation from a crowd of thousands.

Swami Vivekananda

The search for a common ideal in which all Hindu sects could believe was carried on by the Theosophical Society, too, and the Theosophists, led by an Irish woman, **Annie Besant** (1847-1933), spread their teaching through pamphlets, lectures and the founding of schools and colleges.

There was another aspect to Hindu reformation besides its rediscovery of the Vedas. This was the revival of interest in the Bhagavad Gita. The reformation by itself would probably have remained a religious movement. New interpretations of the Gita broadened it into a social and political movement as well. A whole generation of scholars set about trying to interpret it as a scripture that called for action for the welfare of the community. They chose to do this through the Gita because it had long been looked upon by every Hindu sect as the most authoritative book on Hindu philosophy. So the Gita, one of the oldest and most sacred books of Hinduism, became the gospel of the modern age with a message that called for social and political action. Leading personalities like Aurobindo

Ghosh and Bal Gangadhar Tilak—and later C. Rajagopalachari, Mahatma Gandhi and Sarvepalli Radhakrishnan—wrote commentaries on the Gita, and numerous popular versions of it reached the reading public in the Indian languages as well as in English.

So, after many hundred years, Hinduism began to play a vigorous, positive role in the country's life and influenced every aspect of reform. It was the activity of these reformers that led to social changes such as the abolition of child marriage, the remarriage of widows, the relaxation of caste and concern for the dalits—all measures that struck at the heart of Hindu orthodoxy.

Cultural Reawakening and Scientific Thinking

There was a great cultural awakening at this time that again began in Bengal. Poets and writers added richly to Bengali literature. Bankim Chandra Chatterji's famous novel *Anandamath,* containing the hymn 'Vande Mataram', exalted the theme of service to the motherland. Plays were written highlighting the evils of British rule. One that deeply stirred audiences was *Nil Darpan*, about the plight of peasants on indigo plantations. Bengal also gave birth to one of the greatest Indians of the age, Rabindranath Tagore, whose genius transformed the literary landscape of the time. Under his influence, Bengali developed into a modern language that began to express the new trends in Indian life. The movement spread to other languages and there was a flowering of literary activity all over India. Novels, plays and poetry, all with patriotic themes, were written. The works of two inspired poets, Subramanya Bharathi and Muhammad Iqbal, were widely celebrated.

Bengal also produced two eminent scientists, Sir Jagadish Chandra Bose and Sir Prafulla Chandra Ray. S. Ramanujan and Sir Chandrasekhara Venkata Raman were two other great men of science of this period. Journalism too developed rapidly during this time, and by the 1880s Calcutta had two hundred papers and journals, mostly in Bengali.

During this period, the research into India's past by European scholars such as Sir William Jones, Max Müller and Monier Monier-Williams not only gave Europeans knowledge of this country, but also developed in Indians pride in their own heritage. Sir William Jones, a Sanskrit scholar who held a post in the East India Company, founded the Asiatic Society of Bengal. His translation of Kalidas's *Shakuntala* was probably the beginning of European interest in the culture and literature of the East.

The Idea of Nationalism and the Rise of the Indian National Congress

Along with this cultural awakening, a new English-educated middle class appeared in the cities. The old Indian middle class, consisting of the manufacturers and merchants of the eighteenth century, had been largely wiped out by the later economic policies of the East India Company, because English merchants had not wanted Indian competition against their goods.

The new middle class was a direct outcome of British rule and English education. It consisted of men who had been brought up on the literature and history of England and admired the British tradition of parliamentary democracy and liberalism. They wanted to see this tradition at work in Britain's dealings with India and so they started an organization, the Indian National Congress, to put forward their views andclaims. The founder of the Congress was an Englishman, A. O. Hume, who saw a growing political consciousness among Indians and wanted to give it a safe, constitutional outlet so that it would not develop into popular agitation or a revolt like that of 1857. He was supported in this scheme by the Viceroy, Lord Dufferin, and it was given shape by a group of eminent Indians. The Congress came into existence in Bombay in December 1885. Its first President was W. C. Bonnerjee.

The history of the Congress became the history of India's struggle for freedom, though its beginnings gave no indication that it would be anything other than a loyal opposition to His

Majesty's government. It had official backing and government officials attended its early sessions. At its second session in Calcutta in 1886, Lord Dufferin received some of its members as distinguished visitors and at its third session the following year in Madras, the Governor gave a garden party for the delegates.

The Indian National Congress (INC) was founded on 28 December 1885 in Bombay. Allan Octavian Hume, a British civil servant, was its first General Secretary. In 1913, Gopal Krishna Gokhale would say this about the founding of the INC by a Britisher: 'No Indian could have started the Indian National Congress...if an Indian had come forward to start such a movement embracing all Indians, the officials in India would not have allowed the movement to come into existence. If the founder of the Congress had not been an Englishman and a distinguished ex-official – such was the distrust of political agitation in those days – that the authorities would have at once found some way or the other to suppress the movement.'

For its first twenty years, the Congress made moderate demands. The atmosphere after the revolt of 1857 was one of suspicion and distrust between Britishers and Indians. The higher services in the army were therefore reserved for the British, and Indians were kept out of the artillery sections of the army. Whenever there was a conflict of interests in commerce, India's interests suffered and her economic development was held up. There were embargoes on the export of British machinery to India and tariffs for the protection of British manufacturers.

In addition, in 1883, the European community in India started a furious agitation against the Ilbert Bill by which Indian magistrates were to be given the power to try Europeans in court. The Europeans declared that they would not be tried by 'black magistrates,' and the Viceroy, Lord Ripon, was forced to modify the Bill. This outburst of racial feeling made Indians bitter. The Congress protested against all these unequal conditions. It asked for greater Indian representation in the higher services and reform in the legislatures. It also complained against the huge expenses of English officials in the civil and military establishments and of the drain of India's gold and silver to England. The delegates even tried to educate British public opinion about their demands through meetings and the distribution of pamphlets in England. They had high hopes that Britain's liberal ideas would apply to India and that Indians would be given a fair share of responsibility in their own affairs.

At that time, nobody thought in terms of independence. India was a part of the British Empire and none of the early leaders imagined it breaking away. They wanted India's social and political advancement and worked steadily for it, but their patriotism was combined with loyalty to the British. Many of them were awarded honours and titles for their distinguished services to the Crown. Not all of them were well acquainted with Indian conditions. They believed it was the job of the educated classes to govern and did not think in terms of the common man. In his welcome address to the Congress in 1896, Sir Ramesh

Chandra Mitra said: 'It is true in all ages that those who think must govern those who toil...'

The First Nationalists

Among the outstanding men of the age was **Keshub Chandra Sen** (1838-1884) who founded the Prarthana Samaj. He was an ardent champion of westernization and at one stage of his career, nearly broke away from Hinduism altogether. He later came under the influence of Ramakrishna and remained a Hindu, but he was an example of the conflict many educated men of his generation were going through, struggling to reconcile their own tradition with Western ideas.

Surendra Nath Bannerji (1848-1925) was a Brahmin and one of the first Indians to enter the I.C.S. by open competition in England. There was an attempt to remove his name from the list of successful candidates and later he was dismissed from the service on inadequate grounds. He then flung himself into the field of education and journalism. He founded the Ripon

College, of which he was President for many years, and started a daily newspaper in English called *The Bengali*, through which he spread his political views. In 1876, he founded the Indian Association of Calcutta which focused attention on Indian problems and helped to create public interest in them. For thirty-five years he, more than any other man, represented the voice of Indian nationalism. He was twice President of the Congress, and became an all-India figure when, after the partition of Bengal by Lord Curzon in 1905, he organized the first movement for direct political action by boycotting British goods and calling on the public to buy Swadeshi or Indian-made goods. When the Montague-Chelmsford Reforms were introduced in 1921, he became a minister and was later knighted.

Sir Pherozeshah Mehta (1845-1915) was a brilliant Parsi barrister who, like the majority of leaders of his generation, did not approve of mass agitation. When Bal Gangadhar Tilak began to inspire the people of Maharashtra to take part in a mass movement against the British, Mehta opposed him, believing that his method would be a danger to India's gradual progress towards self-government. Between 1906 and 1915, there was a struggle between these two opposing ideologies in the Congress, and the Moderate group led by Mehta won over Tilak and his Extremists.

Gopal Krishna Gokhale (1866-1915) was a Brahmin who started life as a mathematics teacher. A selfless and dedicated worker, he became one of the most respected men of his day. He believed that devotion to the country meant constructive work, not political demands, and in 1905, he established the Servants of India Society in Poona to train bands of political workers. The society sent workers to areas where flood or famine relief had to be organized and did fine work among the tribal people. Its members pledged not to accept government appointments but to live a life of service on very small pay. Gokhale's mastery of facts and figures and his quiet persuasiveness made the British recognize him as one of India's most able spokesmen. He worked closely with the British government during the early stages of the

Morley-Minto Reforms and negotiated with the South African government during the struggle of the Indians in South Africa for human rights.

The new class of leaders also included merchants and industrialists. British rule had united the country under one administration. Railways and postal communications now linked far-flung areas. There was a centralized police system and a common rule of law. These conditions of peace and stability gave an opportunity to Indian businessmen they had not had earlier, yet they were hampered in their growth by the special privileges given to British goods and industries. Indian capitalists therefore joined hands with the educated middle classes to put forward their claims. Among them were Dadabhai Naoroji, twice President of the Congress, and a pioneer in trade and later a Liberal Member of the British Parliament; Dinshaw Edulji Wacha, associated with the textile industry, was also President of the Congress and for many years its chief organizer. Sir Cowasji Jehangir and Sir Manakji Dadabhai were captains of industry.

An outstanding industrialist was Sir Jamshedji Nusserwanji Tata.

All these men were moved by high ideals to work for the cause of India's advancement. But at this early stage, the peasants and the town workers did not come into their calculations. It was not until 1919, when Gandhi entered Indian politics—and suggested that the villages should be the first consideration of the nation—that the peasants and workers began to be part of the struggle for freedom.

The Indian Masses

Britain's impact on India started two big processes which went on side by side. One was the flow of ideas from the West which put Indians in touch with the modern world and started a great urge to reform. The other was an opposite process that prevented India, in the field of agriculture and industry, from catching up with modern times. Both these processes shaped the India we know today. We have seen the effect English education had on the middle classes. Let us see how the mass of the people fared.

The Story of Indian Industry

When Britain became the dominant power in India, this country had a long history of manufacture as well as flourishing centres where goods were produced. The next step should have been gradual industrialization, with the introduction of big machines. Instead, as a result of Britain's policies, India leaned more and more on agriculture. Originally, the East India Company had come to buy manufactured goods. Later, when the British merchants found this competition harmful to their interests, they began to buy raw materials from India instead and flooded the country with their own machine-made goods—a policy that brought destruction to the traditional industries of India. Millions of artisans and craftsmen became unemployed and were forced to go back to their villages to try to find a livelihood. This led to the land being divided up into smaller and smaller plots as more and more men tried to find a place on it, and finally land holdings could no longer support even the peasant families that tilled them. The majority of India's people were peasants and as the peasant population continued to increase, the people lived on the verge of starvation. This, then, was the other side of the picture from the one we have just looked at — of the English-educated minority that was beginning to reap the rewards of British rule.

The early nineteenth century saw the beginning of India's growing poverty. The masses did not reap any rewards and were forced to live in conditions of want.

Indian Agriculture and the Burden of Taxes

The Indian cultivator had always given by way of tax a part of his agricultural produce to the government. Sometimes the village panchayat had done this on behalf of the cultivators in a village. During Akbar's reign, his finance minister, Raja Todar Mall, had made a survey of the land and fixed one-third of the produce as the government's share. This could be paid either in cash or in kind. But as the Mughal Empire declined, and the central authority grew weaker, it could not collect tax properly and so it appointed tax collectors who acted as agents of the government. They were not given a salary but were allowed to keep a part of what they collected for themselves. Gradually the agent's occupation became hereditary and the government became too weak to remove him. It is interesting to note that the first legal title the East India Company received in Bengal was that of 'agent on behalf of the Mughal Emperor' in 1735. Actually, though it was called an agent, the Company was, in fact, master of Bengal after the Battle of Plassey in 1757 while the Emperor had no power at all.

The officials of the Company were in no way responsible for the good of the people, they were concerned only with collecting land revenue. They did this rigorously and often with violence. They increased the revenue on the land and appointed more revenue farmers, or zamindars, to collect it and dismissed them if they did not do so punctually. The zamindars were in turn cruel to the cultivators, ejecting them from their land if they did not pay promptly. This zamindari system was put into effect in Bengal and Bihar, and in a modified form in Uttar Pradesh and Punjab. It added greatly to the miseries of the peasant.

The Zamindari System

The foundations of the zamindari system were laid by Warren Hastings, and gradually its power became so abusive that the East India Company had to take notice of them. In 1793, Governor-General Lord Cornwallis came to a settlement with the zamindars of Bengal and Bihar. This was the Permanent Settlement, mentioned in Chapter 2. According to this Settlement, the British recognized the zamindars as landlords and the cultivators as their tenants, after the British pattern. The British government dealt directly with the landlords, leaving the landlords to deal as they liked with their tenants. For the first time in India's history, the cultivator, who had traditionally owned the soil he tilled, was reduced to the position of a tenant on it. He could be thrown off his own land by the zamindar, and he had no protection in cases of unjust or cruel treatment. The moneylender, who had scarcely been heard of till then, now became a powerful tyrant in the village, because the cultivator had to borrow heavily from him. This was how India's huge agricultural debt began. Often whole families lived and died in deep debt. The peasant became broken in spirit, never knowing how he could earn enough to feed his family, or free himself from his burden of debt. The new zamindar class, on the other hand, was loyal to the government as it benefited greatly from the Permanent Settlement.

The Permanent Settlement also fixed the amount of land revenue to be paid by each zamindar to the government. The amount was fixed permanently for Bengal and Bihar, and later as British rule extended to Awadh and Agra, the government made temporary settlements with the zamindars of those provinces. Each temporary settlement had to be revised periodically, usually every thirty years, and the amount of land revenue was fixed afresh each time, usually increasing at each settlement.

The zamindari system did not extend all over India. The South had no zamindars. It had peasant proprietors and the British dealt directly with them. But even there, the East India Company fixed land revenue at a very high figure and ejected peasants if they could not pay. As the peasant had nowhere else to go and no other occupation, he had to accept the hard conditions imposed on him so that he could remain on his land.

Another development connected with land took place in Bengal in the mid nineteenth century. The British established themselves as landlords of indigo plantations. The peasants who cultivated the land as their tenants were made to grow indigo in part of their holdings and to sell it at a fixed rate to their landlords (or planters). The planters had the backing of the government which had passed special laws to force the tenants to cultivate indigo. They could not, for example, grow rice or some other crop which might have been more profitable when the price of indigo fell.

The many burdens on the peasant in the nineteenth century—the zamindari system, the plantation system and the high revenues which were mercilessly collected—led to tragic results. Between 1861 and 1900, there were four devastating famines in India. In 1878, Florence Nightingale wrote: 'The saddest sight to be seen in the East—nay, probably in the world—is the peasant of our Eastern Empire.' She said the consequences of British policies had produced 'in the most fertile country in the world, a grinding, chronic semi-starvation in many places where what is called famine does not exist.'

The Beginning of the Railways

While the agricultural debt was growing, and the peasants were becoming poorer, the condition of industry was not improving. In order to sell Britain's machine-made goods to India and to buy raw materials, the British began to build roads and railways. The first railway was built in Bombay in 1853.

The British built India's railway system from the 1850s onwards. While the first train ran from Bombay to Thane in 1853, the Calcutta-Allahabad-Delhi line was completed in 1864. The Great Indian Peninsula Railway was completed in 1870 and this made it possible to travel from Bombay to Calcutta through Allahabad. By 1880, 14,500 kilometres of rail tracks had been laid which connected the important port cities of Bombay, Calcutta and Madras with places within the country, thus serving a crucial commercial function for the British.

Cities grew up along the sea coast—Bombay, Calcutta, Madras, and later Karachi—which became centres where raw materials like cotton were collected and sent to foreign countries and where foreign goods, mostly from Britain, were received for sale and distribution in India.

But these cities were not great manufacturing centres like the big industrial cities of Europe. They did not produce anything of their own. The government put a duty on machinery entering India, so until 1860, till this duty was withdrawn, the cost of building a factory in India was four times greater than building one in England.

But gradually during the 1870s, Indian factories were established. Even then, large-scale industries like tea, jute, and coal were controlled by Europeans. The textile industry of Bombay and Ahmedabad, which was growing with Indian capital, was discouraged by the government by a tax called an excise duty. The purpose of this tax was to help English cotton cloth to compete against Indian cloth. Most countries put duties on foreign articles so that their own industries will not suffer, but in India the opposite was true, with a tax being put by the British government on Indian goods so that British goods entering India would not suffer. It was not until 1905 when Lord Curzon established a Department of Commerce and Industry that some notice was taken of India's own industrial development. By that time, Indian industrialists were becoming more and more concerned about their condition and voicing protests against it; it was not until the First World War, because of the demands it created, that Indian industries finally began to come into their own.

The Story of Indian Industrialists

The early Indian industrialists had to struggle against great odds. The most remarkable of these men was **Jamshedji Nusserwanji Tata**, a man of indomitable will, who refused to be daunted by the obstacles in his path. Of the many industries he established, the largest and most important was the Tata Iron and Steel Company in the village of Sakchi (now Jamshedpur, in Jharkhand) in 1907. It was fortunate for Britain's war effort that the Tata works were in production when the First World War began. It was also Tata's farsightedness that established the Indian Institute of Science at Bangalore—the first big step taken towards scientific and technological education in India.

The plight of industrial workers during these times was as bad as that of English factory workers a hundred years earlier. So many people were landless and unemployed that labour could be cheaply obtained and working conditions were very hard. An organized labour movement was started towards the end of the nineteenth century by N. M. Lokhande, a factory worker himself. He established the Bombay Mill Hands Association, and became its first President. This led to the formation of other such associations of railway, postal and printing press workers, all of which agitated against the evils of the factory system and demanded better working conditions.

There were so many labourers around that the factories could not give them all employment and many went to work on the plantations, or emigrated to other countries like Ceylon, Malaya, Mauritius, Trinidad, South and East Africa among other places. They went mostly as 'indentured' labourers. An indenture is a contract that binds the worker to his master. India began to hear a lot about these workers at the end of the nineteenth century when a young and unknown barrister, Mohandas Karamchand Gandhi, took up their cause in South Africa.

A National Movement Takes Shape

In the early days of the twentieth century, a number of stirring events affected Indians deeply. One of these was the Russo-Japanese War in 1904-1905. Indians were smarting under the treatment they were receiving at the hands of the British, and there was bitterness over the European attitude of racial superiority. So the victory of a small Asian country over a large Empire was greeted with surprise and enthusiasm. Now India began to hear, and admire, the struggle of the Indians in South Africa under the leadership of Gandhi, and of a new method — satyagraha — with which Gandhi had chosen to defy the unjust laws of the South African government against Indians and other Asians. Indians felt a growing pride in this effort of their countrymen overseas and Indian money began pouring into South Africa to help their cause.

Growing Discontent Under Lord Curzon

There were reasons for dissatisfaction at home. India had at the time a particularly autocratic Viceroy, Lord Curzon, whose policies were making him unpopular and causing a great deal of resentment. The amended Official Secrets Act of 1904 made criticism in the newspapers a punishable offence if it were 'likely to bring the government or constitutional authority into suspicion or contempt.' People believed this Act interfered with civil liberties. Curzon's Official Universities Act aimed at government control of higher education. And his comments on Indian character enraged public opinion. Speaking on the budget proposals of 1904 he said: '...the highest rank of civil employment in India must as a general rule be held by Englishmen for the reason that they possess, partly by heredity, partly by upbringing, partly by education, the knowledge of the principles of government, the habits of mind, the vigour of character, which are essential for the task.'

> *Addressing the convocation of Calcutta University in 1905, Lord Curzon said: '...truth took a high place in the moral codes of the West before it had been similarly honoured in the East, where craftiness and diplomatic skill have always been held in much repute.' He ended his speech by denying there was any such thing as an Indian nation.*

Curzon did not seem to realize the hostility his statements and actions were arousing. He had greatly underestimated the growing nationalist fervour when he made his famous judgment in a letter to the Secretary of State in 1900: 'My own feeling is that Congress is tottering to its fall, and one of my great ambitions while in India is to assist it to a peaceful demise.' Nothing could have been further from fact, for the Congress was about to enter a new militant phase of agitation, and this began when Lord Curzon decided, on the plea of more efficient administration, to partition Bengal in 1905.

The Division of Bengal

The division of the province of Bengal was to be based on religious majority areas—Hindu and Muslim—and Curzon made no secret of his aim to create a new province where Muslims would be predominant. Starting with Curzon it became the deliberate policy of Britain to create and then encourage the demand among the Muslims for a nation of their own. However, many prominent Muslims opposed the partition and Nawabzada Atikullah Khan spoke against it at the Congress session. The Bengalis felt Curzon was trying to break up their unity and solidarity and to stir up religious differences. Huge processions made it to the streets in protest against the move. Bankim Chandra's hymn to the motherland, 'Vande Mataram', became the rallying cry and so inspired the people that the government issued a circular banning the song in public places. Rabindranath Tagore threw himself into the movement and in October 1905, he led a vast throng through the streets of Calcutta singing his song, 'Are you so mighty as to cut asunder the bond forged by Providence?' Other poets, D. L. Roy and Rajani Kant Sen among them, fostered the spirit of revolt, and thousands attended public meetings singing patriotic songs. Surendra Nath Banerji raised the slogan of Swadeshi. He organized a boycott of British goods and public bonfires were made of them.

वन्दे मातरम्

The First Dissenters

Bipin Chandra Pal (1858-1932) was the most eloquent mouthpiece of the militant temper of Bengal, and his magnificent oratory roused Indians from Punjab to Madras. He preached a relentless boycott of British goods, schools and administration, and started a weekly, *New India*, which discussed the burning issues of the day such as India's impoverishment under British rule, and the anti-national character of English education. In 1906, he started the daily paper *Bande Mataram* which, however, had to close down two years later when the government brought a prosecution case against it. A change came over Bipin Chandra's thinking after 1910 when he swung towards a more moderate approach. Ten years later, he faced unsympathetic audiences when he opposed Gandhi's non-cooperation programme, and his death passed almost unnoticed.

An associate of Bipin Chandra's, and perhaps one of the most unusual men of the time, was **Aurobindo Ghosh** (1872-1950). These lines written for the paper *Bande Mataram* convey his passionate patriotism and his poetic expression of it: 'The feeling of almost physical delight in the touch of the mother-soil, of the winds that blow from Indian seas, of the rivers that stream from Indian hills, in the hearing of Indian speech, music, poetry, in the familiar sights, sounds, habits, dress, manners of our Indian life, this is the root of that love. The pride in our past, the pain of our present, the passion for the future are its trunks and branches.'

Aurobindo Ghosh was brought up and educated in England.

He returned to India at the age of twenty-one to join the Baroda State Service, and, at the same time, began a study of Indian thought. Stirred by the writings of the novelist Bankim Chandra Chatterji, he became an advocate of violent revolution against the British. His first political articles attacked the Indian National Congress for its moderate demands and he called on his countrymen to rise up in revolt and liberate their motherland. He sent a young Bengali soldier of the Baroda army, Jatin Banerji, to Bengal to establish secret societies that would carry out revolutionary propaganda there. He himself joined one in western India to train young men for armed revolt. He was arrested in connection with the Alipore bomb case: a bomb intended for the district judge of Muzzaffarpur, in retaliation for the death of an Indian, had killed two innocent Englishwomen instead. Ghosh was defended by a rising young lawyer, Chittaranjan Das (later to be given the title of 'Deshbandhu' by his countrymen) and was later acquitted. But during the year he spent in prison he went through a spiritual transformation. He retired from politics in 1910 to found an ashram in Pondicherry and went on to become one of India's great spiritual teachers.

Lala Lajpat Rai (1865-1928) was closely associated with the emerging radical politics and became the chief spokesman of the movement in Punjab. He belonged to the first generation of English-educated Punjabis, and in his youth, was an ardent supporter of the Arya Samaj. When he attended the fourth session of the Congress at the age of twenty-four, he was already well known for his political writings in the Urdu weekly, *Kohi-i-Noor,* of Lahore. His career covered a wide range of activities and interests. He started the Hindu Orphan Relief Movement—the first attempt at organized charity among Hindu philanthropists—to rescue famine victims. He spoke about the need for technical education for Indians and advocated a greater share for them in industry and banking. His writings in Punjabi and his short biographies in Urdu, especially of Mazzini, Garibaldi and Shivaji, did much to help in the national awakening.

The Role of the Press

The press played its part. There was intense activity in the field of journalism around this time, with newspapers and journals coming out every year from the beginning of the century. Several of these, either because of their sympathy with British enemies or their outspoken point of view that criticized the government, had to close down in 1908 after the Newspaper (Incitement to Offences) Act was passed, that curbed the liberty of the press. In 1910, the Indian Press Act gave the government even more power to control the press. During the next five years, the government collected five lakh rupees as securities and fines from various newspapers. Over five hundred publications were banned. Among these were two started by Aurobindo Ghosh, *Dharma* and *Karmayogin*.

Evidently, Indian newspapers functioned under the threat of prosecution if they printed views opposed to the government. The English-owned press, on the other hand, was closely allied with government policies and was under no such threat. At a time, for example, when Indian public opinion was united against Curzon, the English-owned newspapers gave him their full support. There were exceptions of course, the most notable among them, an English editor, Benjamin Guy Horniman of *The Statesman*, who walked barefoot, in Indian dress, in Calcutta in a demonstration against the partition. A champion of the Indian cause, Horniman was deported from India in 1919 as a result of his writings as editor of the *Bombay Chronicle,* exposing the excesses of martial law in Punjab.

The Indian press was a very important link in the growth of India's national movement. The first newspaper was produced by an Englishman called James Augustus Hickey who brought out the Bengal Gazette *in 1780. The paper was a weekly and was published for about ten months before it was closed down. The earliest Indian language papers were the* Samachar Darpan, *and* Mumbai Samachar. *When the first session of the INC was held in 1885, it was attended by a number of editors and proprietors of Indian newspapers, and papers like* Indian Mirror, Indian Spectator *and* Amrita Bazar Patrika *carried news reports describing the session and its delegates.*

Through the years, there was a constant battle between the authorities controlling the press and the expression of Indian opinion. As time went on, a nationalist Indian press grew in spite of all these difficulties. It played an important part in informing the Indian public and the world about the harsh facts of British rule, and in rallying support for the Indian cause of independence.

The government was not prepared for the Bengal upsurge. It took ruthless measures to crush the agitation. Public meetings were broken up by force, peaceful pickets were beaten and the press was rigidly censored. But these measures only made the public angrier and the boycott and protests continued. Since open opposition was not permitted, the agitation went underground and became violent. Secret societies were organized and they began to preach open revolution and to indulge in acts of violent revolt.

At this time, in Maharashtra, a powerful leader arose in the form of **Bal Gangadhar Tilak** (1856-1920), who along with Aurobindo Ghosh and Bipin Chandra Pal of Bengal, and Lala Lajpat Rai of Punjab, became the prophet of a fiery new nationalism. Under these men—'Lal, Bal, Pal', as they were called—the younger group in the Congress protested against a policy of moderation and caution. Till now, as we have seen, the English-speaking minority had led the national movement and agitated by means of petitions and appeals to the Viceroy. Tilak had no use for these cautious measures. All they had led to, he said, was the partition of Bengal. Freedom, in any case, was not to be begged for. 'Swaraj is my birthright,' he declared, 'and I will have it.' He was the first Indian to understand the political importance of mass communication. He spoke to his people in their own language, Marathi, through his newspaper *Kesari*, and he united them in the name of Shivaji, the founder of the Maratha Empire. He revived the festival of Ganesh (the remover of obstacles) and this religious festival became the basis for a growing political agitation.

In 1896, plague had broken out, followed by famine and terrible suffering for the poor. Tilak organized help for the peasants and tried to prevent the forcible collection of land dues. For the first time the common people began to identify themselves with nationalist demands. The nationalist movement, so far based on liberal ideas from the West, now began to find its inspiration on Indian soil. It was still not a mass movement, since the mass of the people, the peasants and town workers, had not become involved in it, but it had crossed the boundaries of the educated English-speaking few, and its message had begun to reach greater numbers.

Tilak's towering personality made him a hero all over India and he came to be known as 'Lokamanya', or Revered by the People. In his articles in *Kesari*, he bluntly criticized the high-handed measures with which the government had tried to check the bubonic plague in his province. Poona city had been placed under military guard and British soldiers rigorously carried out sanitary inspections, entering homes to examine men, women and children. The people were infuriated at the way this was done and as a result two unpopular British officers were assassinated. Tilak was charged with inciting this violence through his writings and sentenced to eighteen months' imprisonment. It was the first political sentence of its kind and it gave a death blow to armchair leadership in politics.

A Rift Within the Congress

Meanwhile, the Congress, which was used to quiet, dignified politics, did not support Tilak's radical agitation. Since he could not win the party over, Tilak along with his supporters, Lala Lajpat Rai, Aurobindo Ghosh and Bipin Chandra Pal, was forced to form his own group within the Congress known as the Extremists. The main body of the Congress consisted of the Moderates, who still believed in cautious politics, and its ablest leader was Gokhale. The Moderates and

Extremists both wanted self-government but they differed on how to go about to achieve it. The Moderates still believed in constitutional measures. The Extremists wanted more decisive action.

The Moderates and Extremists began to drift further and further apart in outlook. At the Congress session held in Calcutta in 1906, its President, Dadabhai Naoroji, prevented a split within the Congress with great difficulty by declaring that Swaraj was the goal of the Congress. But the split could not be avoided for long, and the following year at the Surat session, the Extremists left the Congress.

The government, which had been watching these developments, took advantage of this split to weaken the national movement. It deported Lala Lajpat Rai to Burma for six months on a charge of sedition. Tilak was accused of inflaming public opinion through his articles and sentenced to six years' imprisonment in Mandalay, and his followers were severely suppressed. There was a nationwide protest against this inhuman sentence and the textile workers of Bombay went on a six-day strike, the first political strike of workers in India.

The government realized that nationalist feeling could not be stamped out so easily. So it made a move to win over the Moderates by announcing that it would introduce constitutional reforms. These were named the Morley-Minto Reforms, after the Secretary of State and Viceroy of the time, and they were contained in the Indian Councils Act of 1909.

The Morley-Minto Reforms

According to this Act, Indian membership to the Central and Provincial Legislative Councils was increased and members were allowed to be elected, though not by adult suffrage. They were elected by special groups, such as the princes, landowners, the universities and various minority groups. So, although the principle of elections was granted for the first time to Indians, it meant little as it was not a free election in which all adults could take part. And the Councils, though they were larger now and had more functions, still had no power. They could only advise and criticize. In a democracy, the Parliament is responsible to the people because it is elected by the people. In this case, the Legislative Councils were elected only by special privileged groups and they were responsible not to the people but to the Viceroy. Actual power remained with the Viceroy. Lord Morley, Secretary of State, made this clear in the House of Commons in 1908: 'If it could be said that this chapter of reform led directly or indirectly to the establishment of a parliamentary system in India, I, for one, would have nothing to do with it.'

The most significant part of the Act was that it recognized the principle of communal representation, that is, only Muslim voters could vote for the seats reserved in the Councils for Muslims. This was part of the British government's policy begun in Lord Curzon's time, to encourage Muslims to consider themselves a people separate from the Hindus, and to create a gulf between the two. Earlier, the British, having ousted the Muslims from power in India, had discriminated against them as belonging to the former ruling race. In 1843, Lord Ellenborough had written: 'I cannot close my eyes to the belief that that race [the Muslims] is fundamentally hostile to us, and our true policy is to reconcile the Hindus.' The revolt of 1857 had made the British even more wary of the Muslims as they felt it had been an attempt to revive Muslim rule. And as a result of this, the Muslims had held themselves aloof from English education and not shared in the intellectual awakening begun by the English. It was Sir Syed Ahmed, the Muslim patriot, who realized that the Muslims must take up English education if they were to recover their lost position in Indian political life, and, in 1875, won the government's support for the founding of the Muhammadan Anglo-Oriental College in Aligarh. This later became the Aligarh Muslim University.

The government took an interest in the college. Its English principal, Beck, and his successors encouraged Muslim fears that they, as a community, would be swallowed up by the Hindu majority unless they had special seats reserved for them in the Councils. In 1906, the government supported a Muslim deputation to the Viceroy led by the Agha Khan, which made a claim for special seats or electorates. In the same year, encouraged by the Viceroy's response, Nawab Salimullah Khan of Dacca (Dhaka), founded the Muslim League. Its aim was to protect Muslim interests and to ensure Muslim loyalty to the government. Lord Morley welcomed the Muslim League as a 'native opposition' to the Congress.

In 1911, during the visit of King George and Queen Mary to India, the king made two important announcements. He cancelled the partition of Bengal and announced that the capital of India would be shifted from Calcutta to New Delhi. The Indian atmosphere, however, was far from calm and a bomb was thrown at the Viceroy as his elephant passed through Chandni Chowk on his state entry into the city. He was injured and one of his attendants was killed.

When the Extremists left the Congress, it lost much of its influence. It continued to hold its sessions once a year but there was no noteworthy political activity in the country. With the announcement that partition would be revoked, the excitement surrounding the issue died down, and the political scene was quiet when the First World War broke out.

The War
Years and After

Alliances New and Old

India, as part of the British Empire, was automatically enlisted into the war on the side of the Allies. Indian resources and manpower were used by Britain to the fullest extent. Over a million men were recruited for the army and India had to contribute over a hundred million pounds as a 'gift' to the war effort. A Defence of India Act was passed, giving the government special powers to control every aspect of the country's life, so that there could be no public criticism of the war or of anything connected with it. The ruling princes and a section of the privileged classes gave the war effort their support, and the soldiers fought ably on foreign battlefields. However, Indians on the whole had no quarrel with Germany and there was, in fact, widespread sympathy for Germany's ally, Turkey. Britain's attack on Turkey led to strong anti-British feeling among the Muslims. The Muslim League, under the leadership of Muhammad Ali Jinnah, joined forces with the Congress at its Lucknow session in 1916, and adopted a joint programme known as the Lucknow Pact. Among other points, this pact laid down the proportion of seats to be reserved for the Muslims in the Councils. The Congress thus accepted the principle of communal electorates while the Muslim League joined in the demand for Swaraj.

Two Muslim leaders, Maulana Mohammad Ali (1878-1931) and Maulana Shaukat Ali (1873-1938), had been imprisoned for expressing their sympathy for Turkey, and a third, the young scholar, Maulana Abul Kalam, for his powerful writings in his newspaper, *Al-Hilal*. Abul Kalam, using the pen name Azad, urged Muslims to ally themselves with the national movement and *Al-Hilal*, started in 1912, played a significant part in bringing the Muslim community nearer the Congress. So altogether the Muslims were in no mood to cooperate with the government.

With this partnership between the two communities, politics began to revive. When Tilak came out of prison after his six-year sentence, he and Annie Besant started the Home Rule League to continue the demand for self-government. Mrs Besant, who played a vigorous part in advocating self-government for India, became the first woman President of the Congress in 1917. She was an eloquent and forceful speaker, and the government, afraid of her appeal and influence, imprisoned her for some months.

Although the Moderates and Extremists came together at the 1916 session of the Congress, it was not for long. Two years later they split again and this time the Moderates left and remained out, calling themselves the Liberals. But the Congress was growing in strength and becoming more broad-based as a middle class organization.

The violence that had begun in Bengal as a result of Lord Curzon's partition had not been altogether suppressed. There were still instances of it as the agitation for political reform went on. The atmosphere was becoming stormy and expectations were rising again. Britain was involved in the war, but people hoped that as soon as it was over there would be some changes in the government's policy towards India.

In 1917, the new Secretary of State, E. S. Montague, announced that after the war, Indians would be associated more closely with every branch of the administration and that Britain would follow a policy of developing self-governing institutions 'with a view to the progressive realization of responsible government in India as an integral part of the British Empire.' Indians waited in a hopeful mood to see how Britain would carry out this intention.

The War and Indian Industries

The war affected India mainly in the economic

sphere. Foreign trade stopped as the sea route was blocked and the large quantity of British goods that had been coming into India by sea was cut off. India had to start producing for her own needs as well as to supply the government with what was needed for the war effort. The Tata Iron and Steel Works, which had gone into production in 1912 with no encouragement from the government, now became vitally important to it. The government realized that only an industrialized nation could carry on a war, and that in case of any future conflict — and it particularly feared one with Soviet Russia — India would have to be prepared. So it was forced to help encourage Indian industry. Nor could it any longer ignore the demands of Indian industrialists since it did not want to alienate them and drive them into revolutionary politics. So the hundred-year-old policy of keeping India as a supplier of raw materials had to be modified.

An Indian Industrial Commission was set up in 1916. Two years later, it recommended the encouragement of industries by the government and the introduction of new methods in agriculture. After the war, other commissions were appointed and proposals were made that there should be duties to protect Indian industries from foreign competition. Foreign capital should also be encouraged to come to India to help build up new industries. But most of the foreign capital that began to pour into India came from the same old source—Britain—and the duties to protect Indian industries only resulted in protecting British capital. Britain also introduced a system known as 'imperial preference,' by which British goods entering India would be taxed less than other foreign goods, if at all. And finally, the government took under its control the important business of banking and through it exerted great influence on the country's industrial development. So, although there was some progress in the industrialization of India, Britain's economic hold on India hardly slackened.

Political Changes Post War

Within a few months of the end of the war, it became clear that Britain was not going to relax her political hold either. In 1919, a Government of India Act containing the new concessions announced by Montague was passed. It was to come into effect in 1921. In appearance, it was a big step forward towards self-government, as Indian ministers (though still elected only by special groups) were given charge of certain departments in the provinces. However, at the centre, the Viceroy continued to be all-powerful. He could reintroduce measures that the provincial legislatures had rejected and he could rule by ordinance if he thought fit. The system known as diarchy was started in the provinces and the provincial government was divided into two parts. Certain important subjects such as law and order, revenue and finance, remained under the provincial British Governor's control, while other subjects such as education, sanitation, local government, industry, etc. were transferred to

Indian ministers. These concessions were so short of expectations that all the political parties were disappointed. And even before they could be put into effect the government began preparing to pass the Rowlatt Bills—which gave it the power to imprison and deport people without trial, and to control the press. There was an outcry all over the country and the Rowlatt Bills became known as the Black Bills. One of the men who took a lead in condemning them was Mohandas Karamchand Gandhi.

Gandhi Enters the Story

Gandhi had returned from South Africa during the war and had settled down in an ashram at Sabarmati with a group of his followers. His peaceful resistance movement for the rights of Indian settlers in South Africa had made history, and he was already well known in India, but he took no part in politics at the time. In 1917, he went to the Champaran district of Bihar to champion the cause of the tenants of the European indigo planters there. Later, he took up the cause of the Kaira peasants in Gujarat. Now, early in 1919, he offered the country his method of resisting the government by non-cooperation.

The general feeling in India at the time was one of helplessness and frustration. Through the years, there had been appeals and protests to the government with no substantial result. Outbursts of violent rebellion had achieved nothing either. Gandhi suggested constructive action. He organized a Satyagraha Sabha, consisting of men who were prepared not merely to protest against unjust laws but to break certain chosen ones, and who were prepared to go to prison for doing so. His programme was twofold, to fight the policy of repression embodied in the Rowlatt Bills and to support the Indian Muslims who were outraged by the occupation of Muslim countries by the Allied forces. He began his campaign by letting the Viceroy know of his intentions. When it became clear that the Bills would be passed in spite of the opposition of a united India, he called for a day of mourning, with a hartal on the first Sunday after the Rowlatt Bills became law. 6 April 1919 was to be known as Satyagraha Day all over India.

It was the first time people of all communities in cities as well as villages joined forces for a common purpose. The success of the programme was immediate and immense. Now that there was a plan of action in which everybody could take part, the feeling of frustration and despair vanished and almost overnight, a wave of confidence and enthusiasm took its place. Delhi, which had by mistake observed Satyagraha Day a week too soon, was the scene of great happenings. There was a spirit of festivity and comradeship between the Hindus and Muslims, and Swami Shraddhananda, the Arya Samaj leader, spoke to vast crowds at the Jama Masjid. Processions were taken out in the streets, and when they were bayoneted, the Swami, a heroic bare-chested figure, faced the bayonets unflinchingly. The entire country thrilled to these accounts and responded with public demonstrations. In Punjab, two leaders, Dr Kitchlew and Dr

Satyapal, were arrested. A crowd mourning their arrest was shot at and in retaliation, the people became violent, killing several Englishmen and burning buildings. The government, reminded of the revolt of 1857, ordered martial law in the province. It also imposed rigid censorship, and it was many months before the rest of India heard the details of the tragedy of Jallianwala Bagh in Amritsar.

The Horror of the Jallianwala Bagh Massacre

At Jallianwala on 13 April 1919, General Dyer's troops fired 1,650 rounds upon a crowd of over six thousand, killing more than four hundred, and wounding over a thousand in a walled enclosure from which there was no escape. Lahore, Kasur and Gujranwala had their share of military repression, but the massacre at Jallianwala was a turning point in the struggle for freedom.

Indians were sick at heart over the massacre, and at General Dyer's inhuman neglect of the wounded. Mostly, they were shocked at the praise he received in the House of Lords. Rabindranath Tagore symbolized the country's bitter disillusionment with British rule when he returned his knighthood to the British government on account of the massacre at Jallianwala. The faith that real constitutional reform would be granted by Britain and that India would gradually attain self-government was shattered.

In a letter rejecting his knighthood dated 30 May 1919, Tagore wrote to Viceroy Chelmsford: 'I... wish to stand shorn of all special distinctions, by the side of those of my countrymen who, for their so-called insignificance, are liable to suffer degradation not fit for human beings.'

The Congress session that year was held at Amritsar and thousands of delegates and visitors visited Jallianwala Bagh as a place of pilgrimage.

The Jallianwala Bagh massacre

In his presidential address, Motilal Nehru said: 'If our lives and honour are to remain at the mercy of an irresponsible executive and military, if the ordinary rights of human beings are denied to us, then all talk of reform is a mockery.'

The Story of the Non-Cooperation Movement

Gandhi now proposed a nationwide campaign of non-cooperation, that is, a refusal of the people to help the foreign government to administer and exploit their country. Writing to the Viceroy on 22 June 1920, he pointed out that, 'it is the right recognized from time immemorial of the subjects to refuse to assist a ruler who misrules.' The reason he gave for non-cooperation was the unjust peace treaty Britain and her allies had inflicted on Turkey, which violated the religious feelings of the Muslims. Added to this was the outrage felt at the happenings in Punjab the previous year. Non-cooperation was to be launched 'for the honour of Islam and Punjab' and Gandhi urged a special session of the Congress in Calcutta to accept it as its policy. He explained what it would mean.

Non-cooperation, Gandhi said, meant titles bestowed by the government were to be given up. Official functions, schools, colleges and the law courts were to be boycotted, as were the Councils set up under the Montague-Chelmsford Reforms.

The boycotts were later extended to the civil and military services and the payment of taxes. Along with political action, the movement also talked about

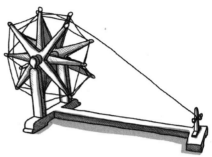

bringing about social and economic change in India. Hindu-Muslim unity and the removal of untouchability – the practice of socially rejecting lower caste people, which Gandhi considered the greatest evil of Hinduism – were important items on the programme. Another aspect of the movement was hand-spinning, and khadi, or handspun cotton cloth, became a symbol of the struggle for freedom. Gandhi included it as part of the boycott against British cloth, and also as a way for the whole nation to identify itself with the peasant who, by spinning his own cloth during the months when his fields lay fallow, could add a little to his income.

The non-cooperation programme, Gandhi warned, would mean severe sacrifices for the people who took part in it, and many of the older Congress leaders were doubtful it could succeed. But the common people had no doubts. Gandhi had given them courage and the multitudes acknowledged him as their leader, naming him 'Mahatma' or Great Spirit. The poor and the dispossessed, whose rights he had championed since his return from South Africa, felt he understood their problems. They believed he would lead them out of their suffering. A new cry, *'Mahatma Gandhi ki jai'*, now filled the air.

The Khilafat Committee (in support of the Caliph of Turkey), led by the Ali brothers, now out of jail, adopted Gandhi's programme even before the Congress did. The Muslim League, although not interested in the whole programme, also joined the movement. On 7 September 1920, the League President, Muhammad Ali Jinnah, announced: 'There is no other course open to the people except to inaugurate the policy of non-cooperation, though not necessarily the programme of Mr Gandhi.'

Above all, the public response was overwhelming. Lawyers gave up their practice, students left government institutions, and bonfires were made of English cloth. When the Nagpur session of the Congress adopted non-cooperation as its official programme in December 1920, one great Indian was missing from the scene. Tilak had died of pneumonia in Bombay on August 1st, leaving a void in the country's political life. Gandhi, one of those who had carried his bier through the huge mourning throng in Bombay, was now the nation's chosen leader and his frail figure continued to dominate India's political life until his assassination in 1948.

The first major clash between the government and the non-cooperators took place during the Prince of Wales' visit in 1921. The Congress boycotted the visit, holding mass demonstrations against the Prince. The Viceroy, Lord Reading, took rigorous steps against the protestors and thousands were imprisoned. But Gandhi had made imprisonment an honour, and people responded enthusiastically to

महात्मा गांधी की जय

their ordeal. A new phase in the struggle for freedom had begun. For the first time, the Congress sent its workers into villages to establish Congress committees, to educate villagers about political happenings, and to enlist mass membership. It could now finally claim to speak for the people of India.

Gandhi's insistence that national leadership should identify itself with the masses brought about an awareness of the conditions of the city workers. Under his inspiration occupational groups like the spinners and weavers formed unions of their own, and scores of other unions were established. In 1920, the All India Trade Union Congress (AITUC) was formed. It became a forum where labour problems could be discussed and it sent representatives to international labour conferences.

The years immediately following the war were a time of great economic hardship and political unrest. Together, these factors led to the growth of a modern labour movement. Workers began to agitate collectively for their demands and there were a large number of strikes all over the country.

Although many of the leaders of the non-cooperation movement were men from the educated middle class — C. R. Das, Motilal and Jawaharlal Nehru, Abul Kalam Azad, Rajendra Prasad, Vallabhbhai Patel among others — political activity had begun to spread to other classes.

The Coming of Gandhi

The Story of South Africa and Gandhi

The man whose entry into Indian politics in 1919 changed the character of the national movement was born in Porbandar, Kathiawar (now Gujarat) on 2 October 1869. In appearance there was nothing to distinguish Mohandas Karamchand Gandhi from a million or more Indians. He was of average height and slight build, with a mild manner and a quiet voice. The son of devout Hindu middle-class parents, he had inherited his gentleness, his piety and his unshakeable faith in God from his mother. He studied law in England, going to South Africa at the request of an Indian merchant, Abdullah

Sheth, who had a case pending with a claim of £40,000 and needed a lawyer to represent him. Gandhi, landing at Durban, set out for Pretoria to acquaint himself with the background of the case. He was twenty-five years old and it was his first visit to South Africa.

From his autobiography, *The Story of My Experiments with Truth,* we have a vivid description of the journey that changed the direction of his life.

It tells us that when the train reached Maritzburg at nine at night, a white passenger entered Gandhi's compartment. He went out again, returning with two railway officials, one of whom told the young Indian he must go to the van compartment as the white passenger and he could not travel together. South Africa was not a country where dark-skinned people argued with officials. This one did. He protested that he had a first-class ticket. The official told him he would be removed by force if he did not go voluntarily. Gandhi said, 'You may remove me. I refuse to go voluntarily.' A police constable was summoned who pushed Gandhi out of the compartment, but he refused to travel in the van compartment as he had been ordered. He stood on the platform and watched the train leave Maritzburg without him. He had to spend the night in the waiting room, shivering in the cold, as his overcoat was in the luggage held by the railway authorities. He took the next evening's train to Charlestown, this time travelling without incident.

On the journey between Charlestown and Johannesburg, the agent would not allow Gandhi a seat in the stage coach, though his ticket entitled him to one. There were seats on the coach-box, one on either side of the coachman, and he was told to take one of these. To avoid further delay he did so, but at Paardekop, the agent wanted fresh air and a smoke. He took a dirty sack cloth from the driver, spread it on the footboard and ordered Gandhi to sit on it so that he could enjoy a smoke on Gandhi's seat on the coach-box. Gandhi refused and the agent, not used to being disobeyed by dark-skinned men, boxed his ears. Gandhi stayed where he was, and when the agent tried to drag him off his seat, he clung to the brass rails of the coach-box. The sight of the Indian passenger being brutally handled by the agent was too much for some of the passengers and they called out that he should be left alone. The agent had to comply and ordered the Hottentot (Khoikhoi) servant sitting on the other side of the driver to vacate his seat instead. But he swore he would get even with the Indian for disobeying him. Gandhi sat stunned and speechless, praying to God for help, but though he was shaken and trembling he knew he could never comply with a bully's command. He left Johannesburg for Pretoria the next day by a different coach and in Pretoria, he stayed with a poor baker's family who needed the extra money and did not mind that their lodger was an Indian.

He had gone to Pretoria to study Abdullah

Sheth's case. He arrived there knowing he must do much more. He called a meeting of Indian residents and told them of his experience. They said they had accepted insults and humiliation for years because they knew of no other way. Gandhi declared it was time to act. They must form an association to present their hardships to the authorities, and he would place his own time and service at their disposal. He urged them to learn English in their own interests and offered to teach those who were willing, enrolling three pupils on the spot—a barber, a clerk and a shopkeeper.

Gandhi spent a year working on Abdullah Sheth's case and studying Indian conditions in South Africa. Indians had come to South Africa when European sugarcane cultivators in Natal found that they needed labour and that the Zulus were not suited to this work.

The Natal government, with the British government's permission, began to recruit Indian labour. Recruits had to sign an indenture to work in Natal for five years. They came as labourers but some prospered and entered trade, building up extensive business interests. The white settlers became alarmed. They felt threatened, and the government decided to levy an annual £3 tax on Indians who did not return to India or renew their indenture after it ended. This was an added injustice to the already disgraceful conditions of their life.

In South Africa, Indians were not called Indians. The Muslims were called Arabs, the Parsis Persians, the Hindus and Christians were known by their religion, not their nationality. And all Asians were known as coolies. Gandhi was a coolie lawyer, Abdullah Sheth a coolie merchant. The word coolie amounted to pariah. The law was harsh to Asians. They could own land only in certain localities and it was not complete ownership. They were not permitted to walk along public footpaths or go out of doors at all after 9 p.m. without a permit. Walking past President Kruger's house one evening, Gandhi was pushed off the footpath by the guard on duty.

Satyagraha in South Africa

Gandhi was to leave for home at the end of his year's stay but he stayed on at the request of the Indian community to launch a campaign against the South African government's annual tax on Indians. They drew up a petition to Lord Ripon, Secretary of State for the colonies, and collected ten thousand signatures for it. A thousand copies of the petition were printed for circulation and for the first time, the public in India learned of the condition of their countrymen in Natal. On 22 May 1893, Gandhi founded the Natal Indian Congress, named after its parent organization in India, and through it, he launched a new kind of warfare which he called 'satyagraha'. The word meant 'fight for truth', and it consisted of peaceful resistance against cruel and unjust laws. One of its chief targets was the £3 annual tax.

It took twenty years of a unique fight to end the tax. Men and women in their tens of thousands were sent to prison for peacefully defying laws. In the final campaign, three thousand indentured labourers employed in the coal mines went on strike, and Gandhi led six thousand labourers from the Transvaal into Natal. Many of these were wives of the coal miners, who joined the march with babies in their arms. Each protestor was given a daily ration of one and a half pounds of bread and half an ounce of sugar. They were told to welcome arrest, to endure abuse and flogging with patience and to quietly go on doing what they had to do. The march started at Newcastle and Gandhi was arrested along the route. Hearing this, twenty thousand more labourers in Natal went on strike and staged demonstrations that police firing could not disperse. At Balfour, the marchers were arrested, put on a train and sent back to Natal where, now homeless and jobless, they were sentenced to hard labour. The march made news in England and filled Indians with admiration as nothing had done before.

In 1914, a settlement between General Smuts, the South African President, and Gandhi revoked the tax. The problems of Indians in South Africa were not over, but one goal had been achieved through the heroism and sacrifice of the people themselves. Gandhi's fame and the success of his satyagraha preceded him across the seas to India. He was forty-six when he finally returned to settle in his country, a man gentle of speech and manner, but with a will of iron, who was convinced that no army, no Empire and no injustice could get the better of human beings passionately determined to be free.

Gandhi was convinced that the freedom of a nation could not be worthily built on bloodshed. It would have to be fought for without violence. His South African experience had taught him that a revolution did not need arms. It needed fearlessness and dedication. In fact, there was no room in satyagraha for fear or hatred. It was possible, he knew, to oppose evil laws and yet remain free of bitterness towards those who made them. He had learned, too, the value of negotiation, that the doors must never be closed on discussion. These lessons prepared the ground for his leadership of India's freedom movement.

Back in India

Gandhi started a magazine, *Young India*, in which he discussed political, social and sometimes personal issues, and through which he prepared the people for the coming satyagraha. On 11 August 1920, he wrote an article entitled 'The Doctrine of the Sword', explaining the meaning of non-violence in these words: 'Strength does not come from physical capacity. It comes from an indomitable will. Non-violence...does not mean meek submission to the will of the evil-doer, but it means the putting of one's whole soul against the will of the tyrant... It is possible for a single individual to defy the whole might of an unjust Empire... I am not pleading for India to practise non-violence because it is weak. I want her to practise non-violence being conscious of her strength and power... I want India to recognize that she has a soul that cannot perish, and that can rise triumphant above any physical weakness and defy the physical combination of a whole world.'

With this stirring and confident call to action,

Gandhi invited the nation to meet its first trial of strength against British rule. It had the effect of making Indians feel like free men although they were still under a foreign power.

In 1921, in order to identify himself with the poorest of India's peasants, Gandhi took to wearing a loincloth. In a biography published in 1923, the French writer Romain Rolland wrote about him: 'This is the man who has stirred three hundred million people to revolt, who has shaken the foundations of the British Empire, who has introduced into human politics the strongest religious impetus of the last two thousand years.'

The 1920s

The End of the Non-Cooperation Movement

The first non-cooperation movement was a great awakening. About thirty thousand people went to prison and for the first time, the peasant masses took part in politics. But the movement ended abruptly. Gandhi had insisted there was to be no bloodshed but as more and more well-known leaders were arrested, inexperienced men took their place. The movement became disorganized and violent, and riots broke out in several parts of the country. In 1922, at Chauri Chaura (near Gorakhpur in Uttar Pradesh), a clash between a crowd of peasants and the police ended with the peasants burning the police station with some of the policemen inside it. Gandhi, shocked by this incident, called off the movement. Soon afterwards, in March 1922, he was arrested and sentenced to six years' imprisonment.

The Congress became uncertain of what step to take next and in 1923, Motilal Nehru and C. R. Das suggested a change of policy. They formed the Swaraj Party within the Congress with the idea that the Swarajists should enter the Legislative Councils to try to influence their working. Under this new programme, Congressmen all over the country took part in the 1923 elections. Several of them were elected to the municipalities. C. R. Das became the first Mayor of Calcutta; Vithalbhai Patel, the President of the Ahmedabad Municipality; Rajendra Prasad and Jawaharlal Nehru of the municipalities of Patna and Allahabad. The new representatives took blatantly nationalist measures. The Poona Municipality, in defiance of a government order, decided to put up a statue of Tilak in the municipal market. The Bombay Corporation and the Allahabad Municipality presented addresses to Gandhi. The Swarajists made demands for responsible self-government and for the release of political prisoners. The Congress entry into the Councils enhanced the prestige and popularity of the party but it was not very successful in influencing the government, for the Viceroy passed the budget which the Assembly had rejected.

Group Nationalisms and Religious Friction

During the 1920s, a number of forces were at work in the country. The chief of these was the Hindu-Muslim question. The non-cooperation movement had been a time of remarkable comradeship between the two communities but once it ended, they began to drift apart. The Muslims had originally joined the movement because of Gandhi's sympathy for the Khilafat cause, in support of the Caliph of Turkey. Khilafat was now no longer an issue. The Muslims, who had opposed English education, were beginning to feel they had been left behind in the competition for jobs and were alarmed at the growing influence of the Congress. They demanded protection and special treatment for their community. The British government also encouraged this rift and seized opportunities to widen it.

The Sikhs were making demands of their own. They had at first been interested mostly in religious questions, in their shrines and the property belonging to them. But when processions of Akali Sikhs were brutally beaten by the police, the community began to turn to politics. Similarly, the poorer, low-caste classes, who were largely landless labourers, and who had been inhumanly treated by the Hindus for centuries, began to assert their rights.

With these group nationalisms coming to the fore, the Congress and the larger idea of freedom receded into the background. The main work of the Congress during this period was the promotion of khadi and attempting to engage itself with the people in the countryside.

The Simon Commission and Further Unrest

In 1927, the British government announced the appointment of a commission to find out how the 1919 reforms had worked in India. No Indian was made a member of the commission and all the Indian political parties decided to boycott it. The Congress, holding its annual session in Madras that year, created an All Parties Conference to draw up a constitution for the country and find a way out of the communal trouble.

The conference produced the Nehru Report, named after Motilal Nehru, chairman of the drafting committee. The Nehru Report recommended that India should have a constitution like that of the British dominions. The Calcutta Congress of December 1928 adopted the report and fixed a time limit of one year for the government's acceptance of it. If the government did not give India dominion status in a year's time, the Congress would demand complete independence.

In 1928, the Simon Commission, named

after its chairman, Sir John Simon, visited India and was met by large-scale demonstrations urging 'Simon, go back.' There were lathi charges against the demonstrators. In one of these, Lala Lajpat Rai, leading a mass demonstration in front of Lahore railway station on 30 October, was beaten and he later died, it was generally believed, of his injuries on 17 November.

After a short spell of post-war prosperity, a period of economic distress and unemployment set in. In Bardoli (Gujarat), Sardar Vallabhbhai Patel led a peasant movement against an increase in taxes and won a victory against the government. There was an outbreak of strikes and in Bombay, more than a hundred thousand workers took part in these. In 1929, the government arrested thirty-two labour leaders on no specific charge and started a case against them, known as the Meerut Conspiracy Case. After a trial lasting four years, nearly all the accused were sentenced to long terms of imprisonment, though these sentences were later reduced.

During this time, there was violent revolutionary activity in Bengal, Punjab and Uttar Pradesh. To keep this in check, in Bengal, a special law called the Bengal Ordinance was passed to authorize the government to make arrests without trial.

During this period, three acts of revolutionary violence attracted public attention. A young Bhagat Singh shot the British officer in Lahore who was alleged to have assaulted Lala Lajpat Rai during the demonstration against the Simon Commission. A bomb was thrown in the Assembly in Delhi by Bhagat Singh and Batukeshwara Dutt. The bomb did little damage but Bhagat Singh, who had become a national hero, was arrested and later executed in 1931. The third was an Indian raid on the government armoury in Chittagong in 1930 under the leadership of Surya Sen ('Masterda'). As a result of this, parts of East Bengal were put under military rule and security measures were tightened.

In October 1929, Viceroy Lord Irwin announced a Round Table Conference, to be attended by all political parties, would take place in London. The Congress meeting in Lahore in December under the presidentship of Jawaharlal Nehru boycotted the conference. At the age of forty, Jawaharlal Nehru already enjoyed unrivalled popularity among the older and younger members alike. By this time, the ultimatum demanding complete independence given at Calcutta the previous year to the government had ended, at midnight on 31 December .

At exactly that hour, the national flag was unfurled in the presence of thousands of enthusiastic delegates. Congress members resigned from the Assembly and the Councils. On 26 January 1930, the national flag was hoisted and an independence pledge was taken at gatherings all over India. The flag, conceived by Lala

Hansraj of Jullundur (now Jalandhar) in 1921, had a spinning wheel as its emblem. To this, Gandhi had added three colours as background — orange, white and green, to represent all the faiths and peoples of India.

A Force Mightier Than Violence

The Salt March

The year 1930 began with a pledge of independence and in March, Gandhi opened a new chapter in the policy of non-cooperation with the government by announcing that he would break the salt law. The tax on salt imposed by the government had increased its price and badly affected the poor. Gandhi called it 'the most inhuman poll tax the ingenuity of man can devise.' Gandhi felt the refusal to pay it would make the people confident and show them they were capable of independent action.

He wrote to Lord Irwin, the then Viceroy, to let him know of his intention: 'Dear friend, before embarking on civil disobedience I would fain approach you and find a way out...the much vaunted Permanent Settlement benefits a few rich zamindars, not the ryots (peasants). The ryot has remained as helpless as ever. He is a mere tenant at will...the British system seems designed to crush the very life out of him. Even the salt he must use to live is so taxed as to make the burden fall heaviest on him... If you cannot see your way to deal with these evils and my letter makes no appeal to your heart, on the eleventh day of this month, I shall proceed with such co-workers of the ashram as I can take, to disregard the provisions of the salt laws... It is, I know, open to you to frustrate my design by arresting me. I hope that there will be tens of thousands ready, in a disciplined manner, to take up the work after me, and in the act of disobeying the Salt Act, to lay themselves open to the penalties of a law that should never have disfigured the statute book.'

Gandhi's plan was to walk from his ashram at Sabarmati to Dandi, a deserted village on the sea coast about two hundred miles away, and to make salt on the beach there, thus defying the government monopoly on manufacturing salt. Applicants from all over the country wrote, begging to be included among the volunteers who would accompany him. But he had decided to take only his own ashram mates in the first batch, most of whom had received strict training in non-violence for the past fifteen years. With the whole world watching this mass experiment in civil disobedience, he left his ashram on 12 March 1930, with seventy-eight followers, whose ages ranged from sixteen to sixty-one. Gandhi was the sixty-one-year-old, and the eldest.

For miles, the roads had been watered, strewn with leaves and lined with flags and festoons for Gandhi to pass. The march was joined by thousands of supporters along the way, and they reached Dandi on 5 April.

> *Jawaharlal Nehru summed up the nation's belief and homage when he said, 'Today the pilgrim marches onward on his long trek. Staff in hand he goes along the dusty roads of Gujarat, clear-eyed, firm of step, with his faithful band trudging along behind him...the fire of a great resolve is in him and surpassing love of his miserable countrymen, and love of truth that scorches and love of freedom that inspires...'*

Gandhi had decided that Abbas Tyabji, ex-Justice of Baroda, would take over leadership of the salt satyagraha from him, and after Tyabji, Sarojini Naidu. Naidu—President of the Congress in 1925, poet and powerful orator—took over almost immediately as Abbas Tyabji was arrested before he could take any action. It was her job to lead over two thousand volunteers in a raid on the Dharasana salt depot about 150 miles north of Bombay. After a prayer and a brief talk to the volunteers reminding them they must not use violence under any circumstance and that 'India's

prestige is in your hands,' she led the throng forward.

The salt pans were surrounded with barbed

wire stockade and ditches filled with water, and guarded by four hundred Surat police with six or seven British officers in command. The police carried lathis and five-foot steel-tipped clubs. Inside the stockade, twenty-five riflemen stood ready. The satyagrahis drew up a hundred yards from the stockade and a picket column advanced, wading through the ditches and approaching the barbed wire. The police ordered them to stop but they continued to go forward.

An American journalist, Webb Miller, who was at the scene, reports what happened next: 'Suddenly at a word of command, scores of native police rushed upon the advancing marchers and rained blows on their heads with steel-shod lathis. Not one of the marchers even raised an arm to fend off the blows. They went down like ninepins. From where I stood I heard sickening whacks of the clubs on unprotected heads. The waiting crowd of watchers groaned and sucked in their breaths in sympathetic pain at every blow. Those struck down fell sprawling unconscious or writhing in pain with fractured skulls or broken shoulders. In two or three minutes the ground was quilted with their bodies. Great patches of blood widened on their white clothes. The survivors without breaking the ranks silently and doggedly marched on until struck down... Although everyone knew that within a few minutes he would be beaten down, perhaps killed, I could detect no signs of wavering or fear.' Miller went on to say: 'In eighteen years of my reporting in twenty countries, during which I have witnessed innumerable civil disturbances, riots, street fights and rebellions, I have never witnessed such harrowing scenes as at Dharasana.'

Miller's report reached newspapers all over the world and during the 1930s, India's non-violent crusade aroused astonishment and admiration, as other countries read of unarmed people standing up to the military might of an Empire with no weapon except their own courage.

Satyagraha Spreads through India

By April a massive non-cooperation movement was in full swing all over the country, with other selected laws being broken, and a continuing boycott of British goods. After Gandhi's arrest on

4 May, there was a wave of strikes and hartals. In Bombay, fifty thousand textile workers put down their tools and railway workers joined a demonstration so vast that the sight of it persuaded the police to retire from the scene. At Poona, where Gandhi was imprisoned, a number of officials announced their resignations. Nearly a hundred thousand people went to prison.

Government repression was brutal. There were lathi and cavalry charges all over the country and the police fired on crowds in Calcutta, Madras and Karachi. In Peshawar, where armoured cars were used to disperse a huge demonstration on 23 April, a car was burnt and though its occupants escaped, the police fired freely on the crowds in retaliation. Two platoons of the Second Battalion of the 18th Royal Garhwal Rifles (Indian troops) refused to open fire on their own countrymen and a number of them laid down their arms. Immediately after this dramatic event, the police and military were withdrawn from Peshawar, and British forces with air squadrons were sent.

By autumn, imports of British cotton goods had come down to one-third of the previous year and sixteen British-owned mills in Bombay had to close down because of the boycott of British goods. Indian-owned mills, on the other hand, worked on double shifts and one hundred and thirteen of them signed a pledge to do away with competition between mill-made cloth and khadi by refusing to produce cloth below eighteen counts. In 1929, there were three hundred and eighty-four khadi stores. A year later there were six hundred.

Women and the National Movement

This second phase of non-cooperation saw the entry of women into the movement, one of Gandhi's most spectacular contributions to modern India. Much earlier, the Brahmo Samaj had led the movement to emancipate women from purdah and give them opportunities for education. By the early twentieth century, education for women had become popular and some women had begun to do important social work, among them Pandita Ramabai Ranade, Mrs P. K. Ray, and Maharani Chimnabai of Baroda. In 1927, the Women's Conference was organized to study the special problems of Indian women and to make social reform a part of the Indian revolution. But it was Gandhi's movement that brought women forward in their hundreds of thousands from all classes and walks of life to join the fight for freedom. The majority of them had never before left the shelter of their homes, a fact that made their participation all the more remarkable. Gandhi was the first to recognize the great untried strength and ability of Indian women and to channelize their energies into the political life of the country.

There were many who became active and dedicated political workers — Kamaladevi Chattopadhyay, Aruna Asaf Ali, Amu Swaminadhan, Mridula Sarabhai, Hansa Mehta, Muthamma Reddy, Jethi Sipahimalani and others.

Three women deserve special mention, both for their distinguished role in the national movement and the lasting place they earned after independence in the country's political and diplomatic annals: Sarojini Naidu, the Governor of Uttar Pradesh; Rajkumari Amrit Kaur, the Minister of Health; and Vijaya Lakshmi Pandit, leader of successive delegations to the United Nations, ambassador to the Soviet Union, the United States and Britain, and Member of Parliament. In 1953-1954, she was elected President of the UN General Assembly.

The role played by women eventually brought about basic changes in the whole structure of Hindu society. After independence, the Indian government changed a thousand-year-old Hindu law code in recognition of their needs and rights.

The 1930s marked the political awakening of the North-West Frontier Province under the leadership of Khan Abdul Ghaffar Khan. The 'Frontier Gandhi', as he was known, trained his people to take part in the non-violent struggle.

In April 1930, when the police fired on their demonstration, the crowds remained largely peaceful, surprising the rest of the country by this example of non-violence from a traditionally martial people.

More Hardship and Repression

The year 1930 saw the beginning of a world economic crisis that was felt in India as well. The Indian peasant suffered great hardship when prices of agricultural produce fell. Because non-payment of taxes was a part of non-cooperation, the peasant masses became more intimately connected with the national movement and began to feel that *their* future, too, was closely connected with Swaraj. Non-cooperation was at its height when the Round Table Conference, announced earlier by Lord Irwin, met in London. The Indian delegates to it were all appointed by the government. There was no one at the conference who represented Indian nationalism. After it adjourned, Gandhi's talks with the Viceroy led to a truce between the government and the Congress on 4 March 1931. This truce was known as the Gandhi-Irwin Pact. With this truce, non-cooperation was suspended and the government released all political prisoners and stopped its policy of repression. The Congress agreed to join the conference when it met again and this time, it sent Gandhi as its sole delegate. The session was disappointing. Each community pressed for its own demands. Gandhi denounced this attitude. He made it plain that the dalits, who had been traditionally ostracized by the upper classes, were not a separate community but part of the Hindus, and he insisted on complete independence for India, beyond caste and creed.

Meanwhile, in India, the government issued a new ordinance to put down political activity in Bengal, and another in the North-West Frontier Province, where the resistance movement under Khan Abdul Ghaffar Khan was growing stronger. In Uttar Pradesh, where the peasants were hard hit by the world economic crisis and could not pay their rent, the Congress advised both peasants and their zamindars to stop paying rent and revenue until some just settlement could be reached. The government then issued an ordinance which gave its district officers powers to enforce payment. When Gandhi returned to India and found that the government had gone back to its policy of repression, he called for the renewal of non-cooperation. On 1 January 1932, the Working Committee of the Congress passed a resolution favouring this. The Congress was then promptly declared illegal and Gandhi was arrested. By March 1933, more than 120,000 people were in prison. The third phase of non-cooperation was a grimmer struggle than the first two. The government was now much better prepared to deal with the satyagrahis. Greater force was used to put down demonstrations and the Secret Service was freely employed. There was a form of martial law all over the country and the government confiscated property, houses, cars and other possessions as it thought fit. Newspapers came under even more rigid censorship. The popularity of the Congress, however, grew as it enlisted more and more members both among the peasants and workers as well as the middle classes. It also began to pay more attention to social and economic conditions. The Karachi Congress in 1931, declaring that important basic industries should be state-controlled, took a first step towards socialism. Independence was not to be an end in itself but a means of ending the poverty and exploitation of India's common people.

This last phase of non-cooperation ended in March 1934 when Congress decided to consider the new constitutional reforms proposed by the government.

World War II, Fascism and Further Divisions

Congress Accepts Office

In 1935, the British Parliament passed the Government of India Act which laid down a new constitution. There were to be elections to the provincial legislatures and a federation between the provinces of British India and the princely states, but the Viceroy and the British governors of the provinces were still to have special powers to overrule the legislatures. The Congress condemned the Act, because it did not believe that a new constitution could have any meaning unless it was made by India's own elected representatives. It was not happy either with the idea of a federation between the princely states and the provinces. Most of the princely states were feudal in outlook and autocratic in government while the provinces were at least partly democratic. The Congress was sure that no progress could come out of an alliance between the two. The federation, in fact, never came into being, but elections were held in British India in 1937 and the Congress agreed to take part in them. Like the Swarajists earlier, it decided to carry on the fight for greater self-government within the legislatures, on the condition that the British governors must work in co-operation with their Indian Ministers and not exercise their special powers. The Viceroy agreed to this condition and Congress entered the elections.

Gandhi had recently withdrawn from the political activities of the Congress to concentrate on the upliftment of villages, the stamping out of untouchability and the promotion of communal unity. He felt that another non-cooperation movement would need greater preparation and that the people were not ready for it. Meanwhile, the Congress entry into the legislatures could prove useful.

The energy and interest Gandhi had infused into the populace became apparent as the election campaign began. Large numbers came out to vote, eager to take part in the new venture. The polling booths were often far from where they lived, and the Congress could provide no transport. The slogan 'On foot to the polling booths' became popular, the Congress calling on the people to go to the polling booths in the same spirit of dedication as they went to the Ganges on pilgrimage, often walking miles.

The election results were exciting for the party. It won majorities in seven out of the eleven provinces of British India. In England, the conservative *Times* had to stop calling it 'an insignificant minority.' The newspaper admitted, 'Its record of success has been impressive... The party's proposals have been more positive and more constructive than those of its opponents. The party has won its victories on issues which interested millions of Indian rural voters and scores of millions who had no votes.'

This election, too, was not on the basis of adult franchise. Again only special groups voted. It was, all the same, a historic event for the country. For the first time, elected Indians took over the reins of government in the provinces, though there were no changes at the centre, where the Viceroy and his executive council continued to be all-powerful. The Congress formed ministries in the seven provinces where it had won a majority. Later, it formed a coalition (that is, a joint ministry with another party) in one other province. The two chief non-Congress ministries were in Bengal and Punjab. The Muslim League wanted to form coalition ministries with the Congress. When this was refused, Jinnah declared,'Muslims can expect neither justice nor fair play under Congress government.'

On 19 March 1937, Jawaharlal Nehru administered an oath to the Congressmen and women elected to the provincial legislatures at a convention held in Delhi, 'I, a member of this all-India convention, pledge myself to the service of India and the ending of the exploitation and poverty of her people…' During the short period that they were in office, between 1937-1939, the Congress ministries did what they could to carry out this pledge. They released political prisoners and did away with the government's emergency powers. They started legislation to lessen the agricultural debt on the peasants and tried to initiate better conditions for the industrial workers. They were helped greatly by the fact that they had the public's sympathy and support. It was the first time elected Indian ministries had had a chance to show their worth and the whole country watched the experiment with interest. The party's prestige grew and by the end of 1939, membership numbered five million.

The Second World War

The Congress also began to be more aware of the world outside India. In Europe, the 1930s saw the rise of two fascist dictators, Mussolini in Italy and Hitler in Germany, who used their powerful armies to bully and crush weaker nations. In 1936, when civil war broke out in Spain, the dictators gave guns and airplanes to General Franco to help him wipe out the liberal democratic forces in his country. The people of Spain fought heroically to defend their rights and their freedom. The Spanish Civil War drew support from other countries, who formed an International Brigade to fight for the democratic cause in Spain. But the brute strength of the dictators was on the side of General Franco and his victory in Spain made the Nazis and Fascists more confident. It seemed there was no nation now strong enough to check the armed might of these two nations and the territorial ambitions of their dictators. Europe was on the verge of another war.

Jawaharlal Nehru returned from Europe with an account of the menacing situation. As President of the Congress in Lucknow in 1936, and again the following year in Faizpur, he spoke with passion against the dictators, and against the weak attitude of Britain and other democracies that had allowed them to grow so powerful. He called for a united front of all the progressive forces in the world against fascism. Guided by him, the Congress began to develop a foreign policy in support of the democratic nations.

Meanwhile, there was a militant group growing within the Congress. Subhas Chandra Bose, its restless and dynamic leader, did not believe in non-violence. He wanted the freedom of his country quickly and immediately, and he did not care by what method it was won. With war threatening to break out in Europe, and Britain anxious for her own security, he felt the time had come to give Britain an ultimatum to leave India. Bose was elected President of the Congress in 1938 and again in 1939. His re-election led to differences within the Congress as his views clashed with Gandhi's and with those of other leaders. The Congress was pledged to non-violence, but apart from this, it felt that an ultimatum to Britain to leave India might lead to disorder in the country that the Congress itself might not be able to control. Leading

Congressmen felt that if the national movement became disorganized it would lose all that it had gained in discipline during the past fifteen years. Nor did they wish to deliver an ultimatum to Britain while it was in grave danger of invasion by German armies.

Subhas Chandra Bose

Subhas Bose resigned soon after his re-election to form the Forward Bloc within the Congress.

In September 1939, Hitler's troops marched into Poland, and Britain, long lulled by his promises of peace, was forced to declare war on Germany. Once again, India, as part of the British Empire, was brought into a war that was not its own. But the mood of the country was very different from what it had been in 1914. This time, India was not willing to let its men, money and other resources be used by the British government without its consent. On 14 September, the Congress Working Committee declared: '...the issue of war and peace for India must be decided by the Indian people and no outside authority can impose this decision… India cannot associate herself in a war said to be for democratic freedom when that very freedom is denied to her…' The statement condemned fascism and the German attack on Poland, and said that India wanted to cooperate in the war effort with Britain, but only as an equal partner. The Congress asked the Viceroy to set up a national government in Delhi immediately, so that it could enlist the people's help in the war, and to grant India independence after the war.

On 17 October, Viceroy Lord Linlithgow replied that after the war, the Act of 1935 would be re-examined with a view to further reform, and that in due course Britain would give India Dominion Status within the Empire. What was more important at the moment, he added, was the setting up of an Advisory Council of Indians which would speed up India's cooperation in the war effort.

This vague reply did not satisfy the Congress and Gandhi voiced the disappointment of the country when he said: 'The old policy of divide and rule is to continue. The Congress has asked for bread and it got a stone.' In these circumstances, the Congress could not join Britain's war effort and during October and November 1939, the Congress ministries in the provinces resigned. Now that its programme of work in the legislatures was at an end, and the country had been drafted into a war without its consent, the Congress had to decide how it would continue its struggle for freedom.

The Muslim League, annoyed by the refusal of the Congress to form coalition ministries, had in the meantime drifted further and further in outlook from it. In March 1940, at its annual session in Lahore, its President, Muhammad Ali Jinnah, called for the division of India and the formation of a separate state, Pakistan, for the Muslims. Thus Pakistan—a

Muhammad Ali Jinnah new word and a new

demand—entered Indian politics. The League said it would not accept any constitutional plan for India that did not agree to the formation of Pakistan, and this gave the British government further excuse for not setting up a national government.

In April, a meeting of Muslim parties (all except the Muslim League) known as the Azad Muslim Conference, gave its support to the Congress demand for a constitutional national government to be set up without delay, and condemned the idea of a division of India. 'India with her geography and her political boundaries is an indivisible whole... From the national point of view, every Muslim is an Indian.' But the British government continued to look upon the Muslim League as representative of all the Muslims in the country, and took no notice of this conference.

A Moral Protest

Satyagraha Once More

Many leading Congressmen did not agree with Gandhi about the philosophy of non-violence. They accepted and used it as a successful way of pressurizing the British government. For Gandhi, however, non-violence was not a policy, but a way of life. He applied it to his own personal life and actions as the only true and moral way to combat evil and injustice. He did not believe in violence of any kind, and he did not want India to take part in the war for any reason, though all his own sympathies were for the democratic nations and against the dictators.

The Congress leaders, on the other hand,

wanted to help Britain actively in the fight against the fascist powers, but only if the British government would agree to grant India independence after the war. In spite of this difference in viewpoint, the Congress turned, as usual, to Gandhi for advice about its next step. His intimate knowledge of Indian conditions was an important reason for this. More than any other Indian leader, he was in touch with the common people. He lived in a mud hut in the village of Sevagram, in Wardha. He ate and dressed like a peasant. He had come to know not only how the poor lived, but how they *thought* and *felt*, and what kind of effort they were capable of. No other living Indian understood his people better than Gandhi. He now suggested launching a limited non-cooperation movement, to be carried on only by chosen satyagrahis, and not by the masses as in the earlier movements. It was to be a moral protest against the war and against India being drawn into it without its consent. It would also assert the right of free speech.

As his first satyagrahi, he chose Vinoba Bhave,

and Vinoba opened the campaign with an anti-war speech on 17 October 1940. He was arrested four days later and sentenced to three months' imprisonment. Jawaharlal Nehru, chosen to follow Vinoba, was arrested on 31 October and sentenced to four years.

Jawaharlal Nehru's speech at his trial in Gorakhpur prison became famous: 'I stand before you, sir, as an individual being tried for certain offences against the State. You are a symbol of that State. But I am something more than an individual also. I am…a symbol of Indian nationalism resolved to break away from the British Empire and achieve the independence of India. It is not me you are seeking to judge and condemn but rather the hundreds of millions of people of India… Perhaps it may be that though I am standing before you on my trial, it is the British Empire itself that is on its trial before the bar of the world.'

The third satyagrahi, Brahmo Dutt, was arrested on 7 November and sentenced to six months for raising the slogan: 'It is wrong to help the British war effort with men or money. The only worthy effort is to resist all war with non-violent resistance...' By the end of the year, various members of the Congress Working Committee, the All India Congress Committee (AICC), and the provincial legislatures had been arrested.

There was widespread disillusionment over Britain's attitude towards India's independence. On his eightieth birthday, a few months before he died, Tagore wrote: 'It is no longer possible for me to retain any respect for that mockery of civilization which believes in ruling by force and has no faith in freedom at all.'

On 27 January 1941, came the news of Subhas Bose's sensational escape from his house in Calcutta, where he had been under house-arrest and which was heavily guarded by the police. He was next heard of as Commander-in-Chief of the Indian National Army when Japan's victorious armies reached the borders of India. But the Japanese campaign failed and Bose had to fall back. He was killed when the Japanese plane he was travelling in crashed in 1945.

The war situation in Europe grew steadily worse for Britain and her allies, and it became increasingly clear to the British government that something had be done to improve the political atmosphere in India so that the Indian people would help in the war effort. On 3 December, the government announced that it would release the satyagrahis. The twenty-five thousand who had been arrested since 17 October began to be released, and on 23 December, the Congress Working Committee met at Bardoli to study the war situation. Japan was now in the war on the side of the dictators and India was facing the serious threat of a Japanese invasion. The Congress was more convinced than ever that '... only a free and independent India can be in a position to undertake the defence of the country on a national scale...'

It was early in 1942 that Gandhi gave up his leadership of the Congress. He did not believe India should have anything to do with the war. At the same time, he felt that the Congress had the country's support and he did not want to divide it on this important question at a critical time. When the All India Congress Committee met at Wardha in mid January, he appointed Jawaharlal Nehru as his successor. There had been important differences of opinion between the two men. Gandhi believed in the village as the centre of the Indian economy, and in spinning and cottage industry as essential factors in that economy. Nehru was a man of science who wanted India to become a modern industrialized nation. But despite their differences, the deep emotional bond between them was revealed in Gandhi's words:

Jawaharlal Nehru

'He says that he does not understand my language, and that he speaks a language foreign to me. This may or may not be true. But language is no bar to a union of hearts. And I know this, that when I am gone he will speak my language.'

Gandhi's choice of Nehru as leader, first of the Congress and then of free India, helped to make Nehru the country's foremost political figure. But he was not Gandhi's choice alone. He had captured the nation's imagination and inspired the youth with his own idealism and sense of adventure. Most Indians believed he was the most progressive of their leaders and that the country's well-being would be safe in his hands.

Quit India

On 7 March 1942, Rangoon fell to the Japanese. The occupation of South-East Asia by the Japanese army brought India to the front line of battle. The country now became a vital source of manpower and war materials for the Allied forces in the Near and Far East, and in the Allied defence of the Indian Ocean. It became all the more urgent to have Indian cooperation in the war. Winston Churchill, now England's Prime Minister, announced that the British War Cabinet had agreed on a plan for India and that it would be conveyed to the Indian leaders by Sir Stafford Cripps.

Sir Stafford Cripps was looked upon by Indians as a friend and sympathizer, but his mission was a failure. The plan promised India the right to make its own constitution after the war. For the duration of the war, it proposed the association of Indians in a War Council. The Congress could not give its consent to this because it postponed independence till after the war, and because it ignored 'the ninety millions of people in the Indian states' who were to have no say in shaping the new constitution. The Muslim League rejected it because it made no definite announcement in favour of Pakistan. The negotiations finally broke down on the question of defence. The Congress wanted the immediate appointment of an Indian Defence Minister who would be able to rally Indians to the war effort. It also wanted the Viceroy to treat the new Council as his cabinet and accept its decisions. Sir Stafford would not agree to these conditions and he left for England on 12 April.

The failure of the Cripps Mission convinced the Congress that Britain was not really willing to part with its power in India. At the same time, the need to organize a strong defence against the Japanese made it vital that India should have control of its own affairs. The Congress felt that the transfer of power to India could no longer be delayed. On 8 August 1942, in Bombay, the All India Congress Committee adopted the 'Quit India' resolution, calling for the immediate end of British rule. This now became a vital and immediate issue on which the future of the war depended, for a free India alone would assure the Allies' success by throwing all her great resources into the war effort. The committee said it would start 'a mass struggle on non-violent lines on the widest possible scale' to achieve freedom, and asked Gandhi to lead it.

Do or Die

Gandhi told the crowded gathering: 'Here is a mantra, a short one that I give you. You may imprint it on your hearts and let every breath of yours give expression to it. The mantra is—do or die. We shall either free India or die in the attempt. We shall not live to see the perpetuation of our slavery.' Gandhi also emphasized the need for non-violence *now*, since so much of the world was being consumed by the flames of war and hatred. He believed India must have faith in this principle, even if it meant holding to

it alone in a war-torn world, even if nobody understood its stand. Gandhi also said, 'That something in me which never deceives me tells me now that you have to stand against the whole world, although you may have to stand alone. You have to stare the world in the face, although the world may look at you with bloodshot eyes.'

The Congress session ended at ten o'clock that night. Gandhi was arrested early next morning. The entire Working Committee had already been arrested, along with the other Congress members. They were taken to the special train waiting at Victoria Terminus. From Chinchwad, Gandhi and his party were taken onward by car, and the others, by lorry. Gandhi's secretary, Mahadev Desai, records in his diary Gandhi's sorrow at the treatment given to one of the Congress workers, Mehta. 'They got hold of Mehta by his hands and feet and carried him to the lorry where a sergeant pushed him in.'

Gandhi, his wife Kasturba, his secretary and a few others of his party were imprisoned at the Aga Khan's Palace in Poona. Both Mahadev Desai and Kasturba died during this imprisonment. The members of the Working Committee were taken to an unknown destination. Among them were Jawaharlal Nehru, Vallabhbhai Patel, Asaf Ali, Maulana Azad, Govind Ballabh Pant, Acharya Kripalani, Syed Mahmud, Narendra Deva, Pattabhi Sitaramayya and P. C. Ghosh. No one knew until they were released after the war that they had been jailed in the Ahmednagar Fort.

Serious disturbances broke out all over India at the news of these arrests. The government issued an order prohibiting the printing or publishing of any news about the mass movement or of the measures taken by the government against it, except such news as was released officially. With the newspapers strictly censored and the whereabouts of the country's leaders unknown, the people lost all patience. There were strikes in Ahmedabad and Jamshedpur and public demonstrations all over the country in spite of the government's ban. These were broken up by bullets and tear gas. Unarmed crowds bravely faced military excesses, including machine gunning from the air. The whipping sentence was inflicted on hundreds of victims. By the end of 1942, over sixty thousand men and women had been arrested.

The crowds now became enraged and began to attack what they believed were the symbols of British rule and power—the police stations, post offices and railway stations. Telephone and telegraph wires were cut, rails removed and bridges damaged. The railway system of Bihar and eastern UP was disrupted for many weeks and communications were seriously damaged over a large part of the country. According to official figures, the cost of the destruction was about a crore of rupees. The collective fine imposed on villages by the government amounted to ₹90 lakh, and most of this was promptly collected in spite of the extreme distress of the villagers. For the first time in the history of the Congress, thousands of its workers went into hiding in order to avoid arrest and to carry on the fight underground.

'The disturbances,' wrote Prime Minister Churchill, 'were crushed with all the weight of the government... Larger reinforcements have reached India and the number of white troops in that country is larger than at any time in the British connection.' Indians listened to Churchill's pronouncements with bitterness. It seemed ironic that Britain, fighting gallantly for her own survival, should so brutally suppress Indians struggling to be free. In protest against Churchill's statement, Premier Allah Baksh of Sindh (whose non-Congress ministry had continued in office) gave up his titles and decorations and was dismissed by the British Governor of the province. The fever against British rule mounted as Churchill made it plain: 'I have not become the king's first minister in order to preside over the liquidation of the British Empire.'

In his jail in Poona, Gandhi decided to go on a twenty-one-day fast beginning on 9 February 1943, 'to crucify the flesh' in support of those who were suffering for satyagraha. He wrote to Viceroy Wavell: '...some day those who have the power will realize that they have wronged innocent men.' There was deep anxiety in the country at his decision and Sir Homi Modi, N. R. Sarkar and M. S. Aney resigned from the Viceroy's executive council as a protest against his imprisonment. There began a countrywide agitation for his immediate release. The Viceroy would not agree to release him, nor allow President Roosevelt's special envoy, William Phillips, to see him in jail. In order to justify its stand in the event of Gandhi's death, the government published a pamphlet called 'Congress Responsibility for the Disturbances' which Gandhi later repudiated as false.

Gandhi's fast ended on 3 March, and to the country's great relief he survived his ordeal. The agitation for his release continued in India and abroad. Public conscience rebelled at the persecution of this saintly man who stood steadfastly for peace and non-violence in the middle of the world's most destructive war. In England, Bernard Shaw said, 'The imprisonment of Gandhi is the stupidest blunder the government has let itself be landed in by its right wing of incurable die-hards. The king should release him unconditionally in an act of grace unconcerned with policy, and apologize to him for the mental defectiveness of his cabinet.' Non-Congress leaders met in Bombay in March to urge the government to set him free and to hold discussions with the Congress. The Viceroy turned down this request.

The situation in the country grew worse due to Japanese air raids and a terrible famine in Bengal, as well as disorder in Sindh where the ex-Premier, Allah Baksh, was attacked by four men and shot dead. Meanwhile, in 1943, a 'Government of

Free India' was established in Singapore under Japanese occupation.

Gandhi was released on 5 May 1944, on grounds of ill health. One of his first acts was to meet Jinnah and try to come to an understanding with him so that the Muslim League and the Congress could present a united front to the British and compel them to leave the country. They met during September at Jinnah's house in Bombay, while the public waited anxiously for the outcome of their seventeen-day talks. No agreement could be reached because Jinnah insisted that India must be divided and the Muslims be given Pakistan before the British left. Gandhi accepted the idea that in the areas where Muslims were in a majority they should be allowed to form their own state within India, but he could not agree to a separate nation being formed.

A New Era Begins

The End of the War

The war in Europe ended in May 1945 (although Japan was still not defeated) and events began to march rapidly in India. The fierce resistance to British rule during the war years had convinced Britain that some changes would be necessary in the structure of the government in India. The new Viceroy, Lord Wavell, announced these on 14 June when he said that the Viceroy's executive council would be re-formed, and all its members, except himself and the Commander-in-Chief, would be Indians. He said that 'caste Hindus and Muslims' would be equally represented in it. The Congress took serious objection to this remark as it was a national organization, not a religious or communal one. Its members were drawn from all classes and religions, and it had never recognized caste. The Viceroy's reference to caste was a bad beginning for any new plan, but the Congress hoped some good would come out of negotiations. It agreed to take part in the Simla Conference to which Wavell had invited the leaders of various political parties. He asked the party leaders to give him lists from which he could choose members for his new executive council.

The conference broke down just a month before Japan's surrender. It was in difficulties from the start because the Congress and the Muslim League could not agree about the nomination of Muslims. The Congress included Jinnah and two other Muslim League members in its list and its five Congress nominees also included two Muslims — Maulana Azad and Asaf Ali. Maulana Azad, who was the Congress President at the time, said his party would not take part in any arrangement that denied its national character, and that the composition of the new executive council must be considered as a whole and not divided into religious groups. The Muslim League, on the other hand, said it had the sole right to nominate Muslims. The Viceroy, anxious to placate the League, took no firm decision and the conference ended in failure.

A fortnight later, elections in Britain brought a Labour government into office under Prime Minister Attlee. With the exit of Churchill, Indians looked forward to a real change in British policy, and Maulana Azad sent a message of congratulation to Attlee, saying the election had shown that the British people had abandoned their old ideas and accepted the new world. Attlee's government announced there would be elections in India as soon as possible and that afterwards, a constitution-making body (a Constituent Assembly) would be formed.

The INA Trial

The end of the war had led to the release of the

Congress leaders from their long imprisonment. It was an occasion for rejoicing when all the AICC met in Bombay on 21 and 22 September, with Azad presiding over two hundred and eighty-three delegates and about twenty-five thousand spectators, three years after the passage of the Quit India resolution. The AICC congratulated the nation on the courage and endurance with which it had met the onslaught of British power, and conveyed its sympathies to all those who had suffered during the past three years of military rule. On the last day of the session, Nehru moved a resolution on the Indian National Army (INA) formed in Malaya and Burma in 1942. Subhas Bose was dead but three officers of the INA — a Hindu, a Muslim and a Sikh — were to face trial by the British government in the Red Fort in Delhi.

The career of the INA is a separate story which does not belong to the main account of the national movement. Subhas Bose, its leader, was, according to Gandhi, a great but misguided patriot, whose devotion to the cause of India's freedom led him to seek Japan's help. His army consisted of some twenty thousand Indians taken prisoners of war by the Japanese. He inspired them to fight under the flag of a free Indian government with its base in Japanese-occupied territory. These men and women were, by British standards, traitors and deserters but Indian public opinion was not in a mood to condemn them. Speaking for them, Nehru said it would be 'a tragedy if these officers, men and women, were punished for the offence of having laboured, however mistakenly, for the freedom of India.' He announced that a committee had been formed by the Congress consisting of eminent lawyers, including Bhulabhai Desai and Sir Tej Bahadur Sapru, to defend them and invited other parties to join it.

The INA trial aroused great interest in the country, since it gave Indians public information about the activities of Subhas Bose, which till then had not been widely known. Nehru was among those who put on the barrister's robes he had discarded thirty years earlier, to defend the INA officers, and Bhulabhai Desai, the leading defence counsel, drew the nation's attention to the stirring role the INA had played under Bose. He said it was the right of every Indian to disclaim his allegiance to the British Crown and join an army of liberation to free India. Public opinion was in sympathy with the INA and the British government had to take the country's mood into account and release the three officers even though they had previously been convicted.

The Naval Mutiny

Another happening that made Britain aware of the country's uncompromising mood was the naval mutiny in Bombay. On 19 February 1946, about three thousand naval ratings of the Royal Indian Navy rebelled against discrimination in their food and living conditions and attacked a number of British officers and servicemen. They hoisted the Congress flag on some naval sloops in the harbour and forced British personnel off them. Naval establishments in Karachi, Calcutta, Delhi and Madras were affected, and ratings — the non-commissioned sailors — flew Congress, Muslim

League and Communist flags from their lorries as they drove through these towns. When the police and military opened fire on the mutineers at Bombay and Karachi, they returned the fire. A thousand men of the Royal Indian Air Force, camped in Bombay, demonstrated in sympathy with the navy. By 22 February, the mutineers were in control of nearly twenty vessels in Bombay harbour, including the flagship of the British Vice Admiral, and had trained the ship's guns on the city. Sardar Patel and Jinnah had to appeal to the mutineers to surrender, promising they would not be punished. The mutiny ended on 23 February. The flaring up of the mutiny made the British government realize that independence could not be delayed for long and that every political party and group in the country was restless for it. A British parliamentary delegation touring India earlier had also cautioned the government not to postpone independence, and in March, Britain sent a Cabinet Mission led by the Secretary of State, Lord Pethick Lawrence, to work out a plan for the transfer of power to Indian leaders.

Elections Again

The elections promised by Attlee had taken place in January, with an overwhelming victory for the Congress in the general seats and for the Muslim League in the Muslim seats, and in May, a second conference met at Simla to try and bring about agreement between the League and the Congress, and to persuade League members to enter the Viceroy's new executive council. When this too failed, the Cabinet Mission suggested its own plan for an Indian government, to be known as the Interim Government, and all through the summer of 1946, efforts were made to persuade the League to join it. India now stood on the threshold of independence, only the Muslim League would not allow Britain to transfer power unless it created Pakistan first. The distrust between the Congress, the League and the Viceroy already stood in the way of a settlement, and the League now declared it would use violence to gain Pakistan. On 29 July, Jinnah called for Direct Action, that is, violent action to win Pakistan. On 16 August,

Jinnah's statement, 'This day we bid goodbye to constitutional methods,' was the signal for a terrible orgy of bloodshed in Calcutta — gangs of Muslims armed with knives, pitchforks, axes and any weapon they could find roamed the city, killing, looting and burning. The riot lasted four days and was the worst ever anyone remembered in India. Thousands of Hindus fled in terror from Calcutta.

The negotiations for the transfer of power went on, and the Viceroy announced he would go ahead and form a fourteen-member Interim Government at the centre. He invited Nehru and Jinnah to join it with their lists of nominees to be included in it. Nehru accepted the invitation and gave his list of six nominees. Jinnah refused. He also refused Nehru's offer to form a coalition government. The Interim Government took office on 2 September, with Nehru as its Vice-President. Its other members included Sardar Patel, Rajendra Prasad, C. Rajagopalachari, Asaf Ali, Dr John Matthai (representing the Christian community) and Jagjivan Ram (representing the scheduled castes). Two non-League Muslims were included—Ali Zaheer and Sir Shafaat Ahmed Khan—and one representative each—Baldev Singh and C. J. Bhabha—of the Sikhs and Parsis. Later Sarat Chandra Bose was also included.

The Muslim League, however, chose to declare 2 September as Black Day and this was the signal for another outburst of communal fury in the country.

In spite of the League's refusal to join, the formation of the Interim Government was a milestone for India. Broadcasting to the country on 7 September, Nehru said, 'Six days ago my colleagues and I sat on the chairs of high office in the government of India. A new government came into being in this ancient land, the Interim or Provisional Government, as we called it, the stepping stone to the full independence of India... And yet we asked for no celebration of this historic event and even restrained our people's enthusiasm... Our hearts were heavy...with the terrible tragedy of Calcutta and because of the insensate strife of brother against brother. The freedom we had envisaged and for which we had laboured, through generations of trial and suffering, was for *all* the people of India, and not for one group or class or the followers of one religion...'

Gandhi's Healing Touch

While Nehru appealed for a united, democratic India in which religion would be every man's private affair, the League continued its agitation for Pakistan. The talk of a partition aroused fear in large sections of the population, both Muslim and Hindu. No one knew exactly where the boundaries of the new nation would lie, and what would be the condition of the people uprooted by the division. People who had lived side by side in peace for hundreds of years became suspicious of each other and lived in fear. A chain of riots broke out in Bengal and Bihar, and later in Punjab.

Nehru and three of his cabinet colleagues flew to Bihar, where there had been a slaughter of the Muslims by the Hindu majority.

One of Gandhi's last great acts was his work in the
villages of Bengal, where the Hindu minority had
been butchered by the Muslims. He and the
members of his party settled in one village each,
pledging to protect it with his life and not to leave
it till its inhabitants could settle down without
fear again. Gandhi was seventy-seven years old. He
worked eighteen hours a day, walking with
his bamboo staff over brambled village paths,
visiting the afflicted areas on foot or by boat.
The freedom of India, now so close, was the
furthest thought from his mind. His ambition, he
said, was 'to wipe every tear from every eye.'
Between January and March 1947, he did a walking
tour of one hundred and sixteen miles through
forty-seven villages, asking the people
to give up their strife.

In October 1946, the Muslim League finally
decided to join the Interim Government. However,
it made it clear that it had joined only to fight for
Pakistan, and that it would show in every possible

way that Hindus and Muslims could not live in harmony together. And on 21 November, Jinnah instructed League ministers in the government not to take part in the Constituent Assembly. When the Assembly met on 9 December with Rajendra Prasad as its President, for the historic task of shaping a new constitution for India, no League member was present. The League had chosen to keep away from what Nehru called 'the high adventure of giving shape, in the printed and written word, to a nation's dream and aspiration.'

The tension between the Congress and the League grew worse, and the two parties were unable to settle their differences. Finally, Prime Minister Attlee decided that 'a new personal approach was perhaps the only hope', and appointed Lord Mountbatten to succeed Wavell. In March 1947, Lord Mountbatten arrived in Delhi to become the last Viceroy of India.

The Transfer of Power

Planning the Partition of India

Lord Mountbatten arrived in March with instructions from the British government to transfer power to India in June 1948. Later, this was advanced to August 1947. Mountbatten, who described himself 'not as the last Viceroy winding up the British Raj, but as the first to lead the way to the new India,' was faced with overwhelming problems. Communal violence was on the increase in Punjab, Bengal and Assam; wherever there were Muslim populations the Muslim League carried on a fierce agitation for a division of the country. With the League blocking every important decision, the Interim

Government could not do its work properly.

There was also the question of the future of the princely states and what their relationship to the new Indian government would be.

Mountbatten was convinced the League would not accept any solution but a division of the country and that the British Cabinet Mission's plan for a united India would have to be given up. He felt that unless some alternative solutions were found quickly, the situation would develop into a civil war. The problem remained on what basis a division could take place. Jinnah wanted Pakistan to consist of six provinces — Punjab, Bengal, Assam, North-West Frontier Province, Sindh and Baluchistan. The Congress was equally certain that sections which wished to remain with India should not be forcibly added to Pakistan. In particular, Punjab and Bengal, which had Muslim majorities but also large non-Muslim populations, could not be given away to Pakistan. If necessary, they would have to be partitioned, one part going to Pakistan, one remaining in India.

Faced with this crisis, Mountbatten drew up

a plan of his own, according to which Bengal and Punjab were to decide their future by vote. The Legislative Assembly of each was to meet in two parts, one representing the Muslim-majority districts and the other the rest of the province, in order to vote. The mainly Muslim Sylhet district in Assam, adjoining Bengal, was to be given the option of joining the Muslim section of partitioned Bengal. The Sindh legislature would also decide by vote if it wished to join Pakistan. Baluchistan, which was a small, specially administered area, would decide through its own representatives. A referendum would be held in the North-West Frontier Province. These measures would make known the wishes of the people. The final boundaries between partitioned Bengal, Punjab and the Sylhet district of Assam would be laid down later by a boundary commission.

Mountbatten's plan was accepted by Nehru because it recognized the existing Union of India and the Constituent Assembly as the successor to the British government, to whom the British would hand over power. Nehru insisted that this 'constitutional continuity' be maintained so that the transfer of power would be smooth and orderly, and above all preserve the essential unity of India. Pakistan, if it came into existence, would amount to a few provinces leaving the Union. The plan was sent to London where the British government revised it. This revised plan did not establish the important point that the Indian Union would be the successor to the British government. Nehru rejected it because it gave the various provinces the right to leave the Indian Union. He saw in it the danger of India splitting up into fragments.

Meanwhile, Jinnah demanded an eight-hundred-mile 'corridor' linking the east and west regions of Pakistan. Nehru strongly condemned this demand, 'Mr Jinnah's recent statement is completely unrealistic and indicates that he desires no settlement of any kind. The demand for a corridor is fantastic and absurd. We stand for a Union of India with the right to particular areas to opt out... We envisage no compulsion.'

Finally, in June, Mountbatten suggested

that Britain should transfer power to two new Dominions — India and Pakistan. This formula would keep the existing Indian Union and the Constituent Assembly intact, while allowing those areas which did not want to remain with the Indian Union to leave it. The Congress agreed to it after the words 'King Emperor,' 'Empire' and any allegiance to the Crown had been eliminated from it, and when it had become obvious that the Muslim League would not allow a peaceful transfer of power without a partition.

To those who had laboured nearly thirty years for freedom, the partition formula was a sad solution and, it was hoped, not the final one. The message that Nehru broadcast to the nation on 3 June, after the announcement that a partition would take place, held this hope. 'Today I am speaking to you on another historic occasion when a vital change affecting the future of India is proposed. You have just heard an announcement on behalf of the British government. This announcement lays down a procedure for self-determination in certain areas of India. It envisages on the one hand the possibility of these areas seceding from India; on the other, it promises a big advance to complete independence... It is with no joy in my heart that I commend these proposals to you. For generations we have dreamt and struggled for a free, independent and united India. The proposal to allow certain parts to secede if they so will is painful for any of us to contemplate. Nevertheless, I am convinced that our present decision is the right one even from the larger viewpoint.

'The united India that we have laboured for was not one of compulsion and coercion but a free and willing association of a free people. It may be that in this way we shall reach that united India sooner than otherwise and then she will have a stronger and more secure foundation...'

The AICC meeting in Delhi on 14 June also pressed for the unity of India and described it with feeling: 'Geography and the mountains and the seas fashioned India as she is and no human agency can change that shape or come in the way of her final destiny... The AICC earnestly trusts that when the present passions have subsided, India's problems will be viewed in their proper perspective and the false doctrine of two nations in India will be discredited and discarded by all.'

The 3 June plan was then put into effect, with Bengal and Punjab voting on the partition issue, followed by elections in Sindh and Sylhet. In Baluchistan, the Shahi Jirga — an assembly of elders who settled community disputes — and the non-official members of the municipality made the decision to join Pakistan. In the North-West Frontier Province, the procedure was more complicated. Khan Abdul Ghaffar Khan objected to the people being asked to vote on a communal question. He also urged that they be allowed to form an independent Pathanistan. When his demand was not granted, Ghaffar Khan asked his people to boycott the vote. Only over fifty per cent of the voters actually took part in it, voting to join Pakistan. Thus East Bengal, West Punjab, Sindh, Baluchistan and the North-West Frontier Province, in effect, voted for Pakistan.

Two boundary commissions were appointed,

one to deal with the partition of Bengal and the separation of Sylhet from Assam, and the other to deal with the partition of Punjab. Sir Cyril Radcliffe was chairman of both and each had four High Court judges as members, two nominated by the Congress and two by the League. The question of drawing boundaries, mainly on the basis of religious majority, raised enormous difficulties because the religion of the people had nothing to do with the many other factors involved. The partition affected the lives and the property, not to mention the emotions and historical memories, of millions of people. The members could not reach agreement among themselves and finally Sir Cyril Radcliffe was asked to give his own award, or decision.

The Radcliffe award did not satisfy either the Congress or the League or the Sikhs, whose homes and shrines were directly involved in the division of Punjab. Punjab was the centre of an integrated irrigation system, one of the finest in the world. It had been designed to serve a large part of North India and in dividing it, the question of its future control and benefits came up, as did the problem of the future of vast numbers of peasants in this region. The award led to dispute over the canal waters, which went on for many years after independence. It was not till 1962, when the Indus Waters Treaty was signed by India and Pakistan, that it was settled.

The announcement of the Radcliffe award made the communal tension even worse. There was a more determined campaign to drive out the Hindus and Sikhs from West Punjab and the North-West Frontier Province, with massacres that terrified the people and started large columns of refugees fleeing to safety in India. This was followed by a violent anti-Muslim reaction in Amritsar. Altogether around ten million people, Muslims and non-Muslims, were uprooted from their homes and great suffering was caused by the terrible killing that accompanied the partition of Punjab and Bengal.

The city of Lahore had a Muslim majority and was given to Pakistan, but its history and cultural traditions were the pride of all its citizens, and its economic investment was largely by non-Muslims. It was also a centre for communications and a clearing ground for goods for a large surrounding area. There was unhappiness over the Bengal boundary too, which, in the end, was drawn quite differently from the earlier division made for the purpose of voting.

Accession of Princely States and Independence

The Indian Independence Act was passed in the British Parliament on 19 July. On 26 July, Mountbatten addressed the princes, asking them to join either India or Pakistan, depending on their geographical position and the religious composition of their population. By the time power was formally transferred, all but three princely states had made their decision. Only Kashmir, Hyderabad and Junagadh had not. Of these, Hyderabad and Junagadh both lay geographically within the Indian Union not adjoining Pakistan, and both had Hindu majorities and Muslim rulers.

The ruler of Junagadh chose to accede to Pakistan. India opposed this accession both because of the state's geographical position and because the wishes of the people had not been obtained. A plebiscite, that is a direct vote of all the members of the electorate, was held and ninety per cent of the people voted for India. Hyderabad began to think in terms of independence, and a group called the Razakars began to terrorize the people. The government of India tried to negotiate for the peaceful accession of Hyderabad for over a year and when this failed, it took control of the state in September 1948. Kashmir was the only one of these three which could, because of its geography, have joined either India or Pakistan, but the Maharaja postponed decision till he was forced to it by the arrival of raiders backed by Pakistan in October 1947. He then decided to accede to India, and the Indian government accepted his accession after the popular political party of Kashmir led by Sheikh Abdullah gave its consent.

A Ministry of States was set up headed by

Sardar Patel to arrange the smooth integration of more than five hundred princely states with India. It was the Sardar's great achievement that he accomplished this task quickly and efficiently and in a way that has no parallel in history. The princes agreed to give up their special privileges and become citizens of an independent India.

On 14 and 15 August, Pakistan and India were declared Dominions, with Mountbatten as India's first Governor-General, and Jinnah as the first Governor-General of Pakistan. British rule came to an end 182 years after the East India Company had taken over the collection of the revenues of Bengal, Bihar and Orissa in 1765.

The months after the partition were a time of heartbreak and suffering for millions of people, and there was a lot of anxiety for the new government, but all this was put aside momentarily as Delhi stayed awake on the night of 14 August to usher in a free India. Inside the Constituent Assembly chamber there were scenes of high excitement. Outside a sea of humanity heralded the event. At midnight, Nehru

The Preamble to the Constitution

addressed the Constituent Assembly, calling upon its members to pledge themselves to the service of India: 'Long years ago, we made a tryst with destiny, and now the time comes when we shall redeem our pledge, not wholly or in full measure, but very substantially. At the stroke of the midnight hour when the world sleeps, India will awake to life and freedom. A moment comes, which comes but rarely in history, when we step out from the old to the new, when an age ends, and when the soul of a nation, long suppressed, finds utterance. It is fitting that at this solemn moment we take the pledge of dedication to the service of India and her people and to the still larger cause of humanity.'

Freedom Needs Guardians

India's independence had a profound significance for freedom movements in other parts of the world. It stopped, once and for all, the argument of whether non-white people were 'fit' to be free of colonial rule. It then became only a matter of time that other areas under foreign rule began to assert their independence. When India became free, the era of Empire ended.

The fight for liberation brings out the best and noblest qualities in mankind and India's freedom movement was no exception. It attracted men and women of high calibre who believed that no price was too big to pay for freedom. But it was different from other such movements in one way. Under

Mahatma Gandhi's leadership, it was fought without hatred and without bloodshed. Its only weapons were the courage and the determination of people to be free. These weapons appealed to the ideals the British themselves believed in, and practised in their own country. It was thus the first revolution of its kind in history, and the only one after which the ruler and the ruled parted in friendship. Because of this, it was possible for India to take the unusual step of inviting its last Viceroy, Lord Mountbatten, to become its first Governor-General after independence.

There are two more points to remember about the freedom movement. First, it was democratic. Rich and poor, men and women, people of all faiths took part in it. Second, it was secular, that is, it was not a religious movement but a national movement striving for liberty. It was the individual's character and conduct that mattered, not anything else.

Today, as citizens of free India, we cherish both our democracy and our secularism. We cannot imagine living in a country where we could not elect our representatives to govern us, and where — whatever our caste, creed or sex — we did not have the right to freedom of speech, freedom of worship and equality before the law. No system of government is perfect, but democracy is the best we know, because it recognizes the dignity of man and gives people ample opportunities to become strong and self-reliant. Nor can we imagine our government discriminating among its citizens on religious grounds, for many religions flourish equally here in India and together they add to our rich national heritage. In the modern world, nations cannot be founded on religion. Today, religion is the private and sacred concern of individuals, not of governments.

Freedom is not a gift. It is an achievement. Like anything of value, it has to be safeguarded. There is no guarantee that a nation will always remain free. And the threat to freedom does not always come from outside. More often, it comes from within. History shows us that lack of unity is a bigger danger to freedom than any external threat. Freedom's greatest safeguard is a united country. In a democracy, the citizens have the added responsibility of choosing worthwhile leaders, of being aware of their political situation and of performing their own duties as a citizen. The fight for freedom is, in this sense, never over. It goes on from generation to generation and every generation must do its job well so that it can pass the torch of freedom to those who come after it.